SLAVE OWNERS

MW00776343

SLAVE OWNERS
OF WEST AFRICA

Decision Making in the

Age of Abolition

Sandra E. Greene

Indiana University Press

Bloomington and Indianapolis

This book is a publication of

Indiana University Press
Office of Scholarly Publishing
Herman B Wells Library 350
1320 East 10th Street
Bloomington, Indiana 47405 USA

iupress.indiana.edu

© 2017 by Sandra E. Greene

All rights reserved

No part of this book may be reproduced or utilized in any form or
by any means, electronic or mechanical, including photocopying
and recording, or by any information storage and retrieval system,
without permission in writing from the publisher. The Association of American University Presses' Resolution on Permissions
constitutes the only exception to this prohibition.

The paper used in this publication meets the minimum
requirements of the American National Standard for Information
Sciences—Permanence of Paper for Printed Library Materials,
ANSI Z39.48-1992.

Manufactured in the United States of America

Library of Congress Cataloging-in-Publication Data

Names: Greene, Sandra E., 1952– author.
Title: Slave owners of West Africa : decision making in the age of
    abolition / Sandra E. Greene.
Description: Bloomington, Indiana : Indiana University Press, 2017. |
    Includes bibliographical references and index.
Identifiers: LCCN 2017003816 (print) | LCCN 2017008803 (ebook) |
    ISBN 9780253025975 (cloth : alk. paper) | ISBN 9780253025999
    (pbk. : alk. paper) | ISBN 9780253026026 (ebook)
Subjects: LCSH: Slaveholders—Ghana—Biography. | Slaves—
    Emancipation—Ghana—History—19th century. | Slaves—
    Emancipation—Ghana—History—20th century. | Slavery—
    Africa, West—History—19th century. | Slavery—Africa, West—
    History—20th century. | Africa, West—Social conditions—
    19th century. | Africa, West—Social conditions—20th century.
Classification: LCC HT1331 .G743 2017 (print) | LCC HT1331 (ebook) |
    DDC 306.3/62096609034—dc23
LC record available at https://lccn.loc.gov/2017003816

1 2 3 4 5   22 21 20 19 18 17

To William Sohne,
whose support made this book possible

Contents

Acknowledgments

THANKING ALL THOSE who made this book possible is no small task. For forty years, I have been welcomed and supported by the Ewe-speaking peoples of Ghana in my explorations of their cultures and histories. Without the willingness of so many, the hundreds who opened their hearts and homes to me, the many who encouraged me to expand my work to include more and more areas of the Ewe-speaking areas of Ghana, this work would have been impossible. I have benefitted greatly from their wisdom, their willingness to share their fears and frustrations, their hopes and dreams, as well as their memories and family records. So it is they whom I wish to thank first and foremost. *Akpe Akpe!* Especially important for this project was William Sohne, to whom this book is dedicated. As a member of the Amegashie family, he was critical in supporting this project. Most families, wherever they live, are naturally sensitive about how their ancestors are remembered. Flattering and funny family memories can overlap with stories unearthed by historians. But information about long deceased family members can also emerge that is less than admirable. In such instances, it is not surprising that living family members find these revelations embarrassing and then seek to distance themselves from the ignoble actions of their ancestors by keeping such information out of the public eye. I salute William Sohne for resisting this impulse. And I thank him as well for sharing with me his own genealogical work on the Amegashie/Quist family. My interactions with members of the Tamakloe family have been equally positive. I thank them, especially Christian Nani Tamakloe, for also sharing with me the memories they have passed from generation to generation, as well as copies of the various legal documents, and the genealogical work they have done themselves on their own ancestor. Again, *aka akpe.*

From the mid-nineteenth century to the early twentieth century, German missionaries associated with the Norddeutsche Missionsgesellschaft (NDMG) were present in a number of different Ewe-speaking communities in what is now southern Ghana and Togo. Throughout this period, they recorded and published their observations about the peoples, cultures, economies, and histories of the communities in which they lived. Professional translations of these writings have been critical for this study. For this work, I am especially grateful to Nadia Rodriquez, Anna Horakova, Timothy Haupt, Svenja Müller, Marissa Nederhouser, Sean Franzel, Chris Muenzen, Aife Naughton, Kelsey Dow, and Patrick Vacca. Gaining access to these documents often proved to be particularly challenging.

The NDMG that operated in what is now south-eastern Ghana was a relatively small, underfunded organization in the mid-nineteenth and early twentieth century. Often archival and library holdings of their publications are incomplete. Yet, I received wonderful support from various libraries and librarians as I sought to locate different materials both published and unpublished. Accordingly, I wish to thank for their wonderful support, Cornell University's Interlibrary loan staff; the University of Ghana's Balme Library Reference Librarian, Daniel Opoku; my colleague and friend Larry Yarak, who with Daniel Opoku located (and rescued from possible destruction) some of the NDMG publications held at Balme Library; and the National Humanities Center, which provided incredible support with regard to library and archival resources, as well as editing, office, and IT support during the spring term of 2015.

In preparing this work for publication, I shared drafts of different chapters with a number individuals and groups. Among these, are attendees of the Cornell University History Department Comparative History Colloquium, the Institute for Advanced Studies in Berlin, Germany, the 2015 Cornell University Mellon Diversity Seminar, and the 2015 National Humanities Center seminar on Memory (organized by Ann Gold). Trevor Getz and an anonymous reviewer read the entire manuscript. I am most grateful for their comments. All have provided very useful feedback, although I, of course, am solely responsible for all interpretations presented here.

SLAVE OWNERS OF WEST AFRICA

Introduction

A FOREIGN POWER extends its rule over the community in which you live. What would you do? How would you respond? Resistance? But in what form and for how long? Acceptance of and adaptation to the new status quo? But what does that entail? Cautious optimism when that foreign power states it will rectify long-standing grievances? Wariness because of the possibility of unfulfilled promises? These are the questions that West Africans faced in the nineteenth and early twentieth century. By the end of World War One, most everyone in the entire region found themselves colonized by either France, Britain, Germany, or Portugal. And with colonization came the imposition of laws that impacted the very structures that had governed their lives. Local political institutions and practices were altered or abolished; communities found themselves governed by individuals who were often imposed upon them, individuals who would have not been considered even remotely legitimate in such positions in the past. Certain cultural practices suddenly became illegal. European missionaries who had operated in the area only with the permission of a community's leaders, were now perceived as not only proselytizers of a new religion, but individuals whose activities—no matter how objectionable—had the backing of an imperial power that too often took little notice of local concerns. At the same time, novel opportunities emerged. Those who had felt oppressed by the very order that others sought to defend—some women, young people, strangers, and the enslaved—assessed and at times embraced the changes that the new order introduced. Innumerable studies have documented how West Africans responded to the early years of colonial rule. They offered, individually and collectively, simultaneously and in sequence, resistance, accommodation, manipulation of the new institutions imposed, withdrawal from the colonial orbit of control, and engagement to take full advantage of the opportunities associated with colonialism.[1] Of particular concern here is how West Africans responded to one particular aspect of colonial rule: the abolition of slavery.

On Responses to Colonial Abolition: Former Slaves and Former Masters

Prior to colonization, West Africans of every social status had long expressed sentiments that recognized the cruelty associated with slavery and the slave trade. Such sentiments are evident in the songs, proverbs, and life histories that have been collected from different individuals and communities. They are present as well in the confessions that nineteenth century political leaders made when confronted by ant-slavery activists.[2] Yet it was European colonization that eventually brought abolition to West Africa. The passage and implementation of the laws that made slaveholding illegal came slowly. But come they did. Over time, they affected much of West Africa. On hearing about these new laws, the response was immediate. Enslaved women, men, and children returned to their homes if they could. Others renegotiated, on their own or through the new colonial courts, the ties that linked them with their former owners. Still others emigrated to wherever they could take advantage of new economic opportunities.[3] Slave owners did not stand on the side while all this was occurring. They, too, responded. Many sent letters and petitions objecting to the abolition of slavery. A few threatened armed rebellion or indicated they would relocate themselves and their property outside the areas claimed by the European colonizers. Some used violence to recapture or keep slaves from leaving. Others used the colonial court system to retain what they considered to be their property. Many, however, opted to adapt to the new order. They redefined their former slaves as subordinate kin in ways that encouraged the newly freed to continue to associate with their former owners as laborers and political allies. They gave them land. They allowed them to manage the marriages of their own children, the burials of their dead. A few even emancipated their slaves before the European-imposed laws came into effect or provided them with opportunities to gain greater social and economic independence.[4]

The actions taken by both former slaves and former slave owners have been well documented. But questions remain. Why did certain individuals pursue one path and not another? What options were available to both the enslaved and their owners? What constraints influenced their decisions? Why did some among the enslaved, for example, choose to leave while others decided to remain where they were? Why did some slave owners opt to resist violently when others followed a less confrontational path? And equally important, what impact did these decisions have decades later on social relations in Africa today? These questions, as they pertain to the enslaved, have been extensively discussed by a number of scholars. Roberts and Miers noted in their study of the end of slavery in Africa that:

> Freed slaves had three broad options. They could leave their former owners and move away; they could remain near them but sever ties to the extent that this was possible or desirable; or they could remain in their owners' households or villages but on different terms. . . .
>
> For those who moved away from their former owners but did not return to their homelands, the crucial variable was whether they could get access to land and other vital resources. . . .
>
> The second . . . option [was exercised by those] where land [in the immediate area] was easy to acquire . . . where [slaves could get away with insisting]

they were now working for themselves . . . [and where] chiefs and district officers . . . welcomed newcomers, who enlarged their tax base. . . .

The last option . . . continued dependence . . . offered the officially freed a web of security, and in some cases, social standing, in return for very minor tasks such as cooking at festivals and acknowledging their dependent status.[5]

These broad generalizations are very helpful in understanding the objective considerations that the formerly enslaved factored into their decisions when determining how they would proceed with their lives after abolition. But it is also clear that more intimate and personal factors played an equally important role. Evidence of this is found in Marcia Wright's *Strategies of Slaves and Women*. She notes that how women slaves responded to their enslavement was a function of several factors: their gender, their personality, their age, their social background. And in my own analysis of the biography of the enslaved boy, Yosef Famfantor, I document how his experience as an orphan and debt pawn well before he was enslaved by the hostile forces that invaded his hometown, had a profound influence on how he approached the decision to return home or remain in the place where he had been enslaved for seventeen years.[6] These studies offer a quite comprehensive understanding of how the formerly enslaved handled the abolition of slavery in Africa.

Less well known is how former slave owners responded. Yes, we know they used petitions, letters, and the colonial court system to oppose abolition. They threatened rebellion and relocation. They also used violence. Eventually, most adapted to the changed situation. And they did so for obvious reasons: they sought to defend, or at least preserve in at least modified form, as best they could, the preexisting political, economic, and social order that had brought them so much success. What we do not know is why specific slave owners chose to handle abolition as they did. Why did some choose to use violence to maintain the institution of slavery, while others accepted abolition and simply allowed their slaves to assert their freedom? Why did some incorporate the formerly enslaved into their families as kin, but then refuse to view them as equals? Why did still others insist that the newly freed be given the same kind of respect associated with the freeborn? Who were these slave owners? We know their social identities. They included both women and men, religious leaders (priests and imams), as well as wealthy famers and businessmen. Childless adults bought children to raise as their own. Men bought women to serve as their wives. The enslaved themselves, those few individuals who had managed to obtain wealth and status, also owned slaves, as did Western-educated Africans who felt they too could not prosper without the use of enslaved labor. But we still know too little about them. What personal experiences, what individual proclivities influenced how they handled abolition in addition to their concerns about their economic, political, and social standings?

This book seeks to answer these questions by exploring the lives of three individuals who lived in what is now southeastern Ghana between the mid-nineteenth and early twentieth century. All three were deeply involved in the business of trade and were prominent within their individual communities. All were considered wealthy. They had multiple wives and many dependents, including numerous slaves. All took particularly interesting and quite different stances on the issue of slavery and its criminalization. The first two, Amegashie Afeku and Nyaho Tamakloe, were born and raised in the coastal polity of Anlo. Both became prominent political and religious leaders. They were well respected as individuals, and both were major slave owners. They shared in common the ability to take advantage of the social, political, and economic opportunities that came their way. And they were unrelenting in their efforts to shape their polity's response to European colonial rule and its abolitionist policies. This, however, is where the similarities end. As a slaveholder, Amegashie refused to accept the abolition of slavery as the new law of the land. He sent armed men to attack former slaves who tried to return home; he relocated his own slaves to an area outside British colonial jurisdiction. Placed on trial in the colonial courts for slave dealing, he refused to acknowledge either the unethical or illegal practice of slavery. When he was eventually forced to accept the fact that he could no longer exercise control over those he once owned, he and some of his descendants redefined his former slaves as "subordinate kin." In doing so, however, they maintained the social boundary that distinguished his direct descendants from those he had once owned. Why? What motivated him to take this approach? Tamakloe, on the other hand, a man from the same community as Amegashie, followed a very different path. He, like Amegashie, never formally freed his slaves, but he gave them the kinds of opportunities and a degree of respect that eluded many in Anlo, even those who could claim to be of free descent. He made it possible for his former slaves to obtain Western education at a time when such training had become the key to social and economic mobility. He championed the official titling of those who served as the leaders, *hanuawo*, of his many slave villages. Once they were recognized as such, Tamakloe's former slave heads were able to voice their opinions and participate as equals in the governing body that made decisions on behalf of the entire Anlo polity. Why did he do this? The third biographical sketch describes yet another approach to the issue of abolition by a slave owner. This one focuses on the life of Noah Yawo, a citizen of the polity of Ho, located some 115 kilometers north of the Anlo coast. Like Amegashie and Tamakloe, Yawo was a businessman. He engaged in farming as well, but his wealth came largely from trade. By 1867 he had the financial resources not only to buy slaves in the local market, but also to marry and maintain three wives. Six years later, however, in 1873, he made a commitment to give it all up. He vowed to free his slaves upon his conversion to Christianity, and, in 1877, he did just that. Why did he do this?

The missionary society that had encouraged him to convert did not demand this of him, nor did other Christian slave owners give up their own slaves. So why did Noah? This book will address these questions by focusing on the range of factors that influenced the decisions of these individuals. It will examine how they responded to the obvious threat that abolition brought to their economic, political, and social interests, but it will also explore their personal concerns, as these too influenced the decisions they made.

Exploring the lives of just three individuals certainly cannot tell us everything about the hundreds of thousands of slave owners in nineteenth- and early twentieth-century West Africa. But their lives reveal a great deal. As indicated, their actions were hardly unique. Amegashie was far from alone in resorting to violence, nor was he unusual in eventually absorbing his former slaves into his family as "subordinate kin." In fact, with regard to the latter actions, he was typical.[7] A few were also like Tamakloe. They championed through their actions the idea that the enslaved should be treated as equals and given the opportunity to contribute to the success of the larger society. Others, like Noah Yawo, became convinced, for religious and ethical reasons, that they could no longer participate in the practice of slavery. By analyzing not just what these individuals did, but *why* they took these particular approaches to slavery and its abolition, these sketches bring to life the complexities that made it possible for slave owners to make such different decisions about how they would handle the massive disruptions that accompanied the colonial abolition of slavery. We see their socialization, where their ideas came from, and how they responded to particular circumstances and events. These portraits humanize. They captivate our imaginations. But they can also be horrifying. We see them respond at times with great subtlety, and at other times with violent rage to abolition. Some devised innovative means to maintain their privileges. Others embraced abolition even though it forced them to establish a totally new foundation upon which to demand respect and obtain status in their communities.[8] Only by exploring both their interior and exterior lives, the personal as well as the economic and political, can one understand why West Africa's slave owners responded to abolition as they did. More importantly, their decisions have continued to influence to this day the norms that govern relations between the descendants of former masters and former slaves.

Recent studies on the social legacy of slavery in late twentieth- and twenty-first-century West Africa reveal that in many places major changes have taken place since abolition in former master/former slave relations. In some locations, families and communities no longer force the descendants of the formerly enslaved to suffer social or economic disadvantages. In other places, however, the traditional social hierarchy that governed master-slave relations continues to dictate who gets access to what kinds of lands, who can marry whom, who is eligible to hold certain political leadership positions, who is to be taken seriously as a religious leader. The studies that have examined these particular legacies tend to focus almost exclusively on those areas where the memories of slave origins still impact daily life, and where the descendants of the enslaved have formed movements to circumvent the restrictions that are still being placed upon them.[9] This is not the situation in what is now Ghana, where the three individuals whose biographies are outlined here lived, worked, and possessed slaves. There is no evidence that slave origins alone have prevented a whole class of people from prospering on the local, regional, or national level in Ghana. They do not influence marital decisions. They have no influence on economic opportunities. Access to schooling—made available to slave and free alike during the colonial and postcolonial periods—rendered slave origins largely irrelevant. Migration for economic reasons to other areas made questions of one's distant origins, at home and abroad, far less important for measuring social status than the rewards one could accrue from such experiences. What accounts for this? Can one attribute it to the less hierarchical character of Ghanaian society in comparison with other areas within West Africa where the social stigma of social origins has remained so strong? Or is it associated with the inability of former slave masters to maintain their privileged positions given the relatively wide distribution of economic opportunities that emerged first in the colonial period? Did the existence of a long-standing educated elite that opted, once abolition had occurred, to downplay differences within the population so as to build an inclusive anticolonial, nationalist political culture in what is now Ghana make a difference? It is probably impossible to answer these questions. How do you explain what did *not* happen? A more fruitful approach is to analyze what *did* happen. What are the legacies of the many individual decisions that slave owners took long ago on how to respond to slavery? How did these individual decisions coalesce into a more general approach within their communities? It is these questions that I will explore in the epilogues to each of the three biographies discussed here.

On Writing Slave Owners' Biographies: Politics, Ethics, and Emotions

Biographies of West Africa's nineteenth-century slave owners are rare.[10] Scholars find that documentary sources about a particular area often contain far too little information to reconstruct a reasonably full picture of a person's experiences and deeds, let alone his or her thoughts and feelings. Oral sources can be helpful, but they, too, can be quite fragmentary. If one is lucky enough to find sufficient information in both the oral and written sources, one must still grapple with the existence of biases and informational lapses. These are issues that historians of Africa have long encountered in their efforts to understand the African past, but they are especially acute when attempting to write about the lives of specific individuals. The few biographies of slaveholders that do exist tend to shy away from focusing specifically on their ownership of slaves. The reasons for this are many. In the 1990s when I was conducting research on slavery in southeastern Ghana, I found that the descendants of slave owners were more than willing to discuss the status and wealth of their ancestors. They recounted with pride the large number of slaves their ancestors could rely on to carry out every conceivable task. They remembered that this number used to be publicly displayed as cowries strung around the central pillar of a stool. Yet, when asked to identify those families whose ancestors belonged to particular slave owners, answers were rarely forthcoming.[11] Customary law and social norms now forbid the public discussion of such information. As one individual from the coastal polity of Anlo in southeastern Ghana noted in 1987:

> If someone refers to your slave as such, they threaten the prosperity of the family who owns the slave and the clan of that family. It is a serious matter. No court will allow it. No elder will bring [a] case [that allows such information to be used]. If you don't know and you try it, you will be revealing the secrets of the families in town and they will form a gang and you will disappear immediately. They will kill you spiritually, instantly. It is not done.[12]

What *could* be revealed were generalities: the sources of an ancestor's wealth in slaves (from warfare and/or trade), the existence of benign treatment and the generous considerations the slave owner gave to the enslaved. Memories about specific master/slave interactions, how the owner interacted with his or her slaves, what that ancestor thought about abolition, were often lost to the passage of time. Documentary sources often are no better. Under such circumstances, constructing biographies of slave owners that focus specifically on their roles as slave masters can be quite challenging.

Equally important is the fact that many historians would probably be reluctant to construct slave owner biographies even if sources were available. The topic itself runs counter to much of the political orientation of the field. Historian Ibrahima Thioub explains:

> Following the Second World War, in a context marked by . . . nationalist and Pan-Africanist movement[s], Africans [and many Westerners who] engaged in academic writing about the continent . . . [sought to] re-establish an African historical consciousness [that had been distorted] by colonial ideology. [This ideology] developed directly from the racist ideas that, in the 18th century, legitimized the Atlantic slave trade. The task [of the historian of Africa at that time] was to give the nationalist movement a past worthy of its ambitions. The solution was to . . . connect the precolonial past with the coming liberation [from colonial rule] by bracketing [off the inglorious history of the slave trade, and] . . . colonization. This enterprise . . . arrived at a glorious history for Africa by erasing more or less systematically everything that could support ideas [about] . . . the backwardness of [African societies]. . . . A 'black' Africa was invented . . . the cradle of a civilization of harmony and equilibrium,

of a humanity reflected in its institutions and elsewhere, with no equal in grandeur. . . . [Under this kind of influence] domestic slavery [ceased] to have a history.[13]

In the 1970s, with the emergence of social history, many Western and some African historians of Africa began to move away from this nationalist-inflected approach that celebrated only what in the African past could be defined as positive and worthy of celebration. They began to explore the history of a number of previously ignored groups who suffered not just from colonial oppression, but who had also been marginalized by the social and political hierarchies within their own local African communities. Historical studies that had once focused almost exclusively on elite men, began to be superseded by those that examined, or at least included, women of all backgrounds (queen mothers, prostitutes, the elderly, and ordinary, average women farmers and traders), ethnic outsiders, youth, and the disabled. Studies of slavery in Africa blossomed as well. And where sources allowed, scholars also produced biographies and life histories of the enslaved.[14] Virtually nothing, however, was written about those elites who benefitted politically, economically, and socially from the institution: how they thought about, understood, and experienced slavery as slave owners; why they chose to oppose, acquiesce, or embrace its abolition. The greater concern to focus on excavating the histories of the invisible and the voiceless, those who were often at the center of change, not as major power brokers but as subaltern actors, explains some of this. To examine the lives of the powerful and influential has run counter to a long-standing focus on Africa's subalterns. But it can also be attributed to the lingering grip of nationalism on scholars of Africa, both Western and African.

Just as historians found it quite important in the 1950s and '60s to counter racist notions about Africa by documenting the continent's long history of state formation, the existence of mutually beneficial trade relations with other parts of the world well before the Atlantic slave trade, and the value of using oral sources to reconstruct the past, so, too, have they continued to feel the need in subsequent decades to present a positive image of the continent. This was especially true in the 1970s, '80s, and '90s as the political, economic, and ecological difficulties faced by many African countries during this period allowed Western journalists to produce images of an undifferentiated continent mired in seemingly self-inflicted poverty, corruption, and war, afflicted by cultural practices defined ethnocentrically as bizarre and inexplicable. Such images continue to dominant world media in the twenty-first century. It is no wonder, then, that few studies focus on the biographies of slave owners. Such studies have the potential to present yet another set of negative images of Africa and Africans. It was Africans, slave owners within the continent, who opposed the abolition of slavery. It was they who were the oppressors, while the Western colonizers were theoretically on the side of the oppressed. Few historians have chosen to enter the territory of slave owner biographical writing, fraught as it is with these past and present political concerns.

An additional factor that has likely given historians pause about writing the biographies of slave owners that discuss slavery as central to their identities has to do with the issue of social origins. As noted above, a slave background remains a stigma in much of West Africa. Few are prepared to discuss it publically. Yet many slave owners themselves were the descendants of enslaved individuals. This creates a dilemma for the historian. How does one discuss this aspect of a slave owner's life when revealing that person's slave origins is considered taboo? One solution is simply to omit that information. Historians make decisions all the time about what to include and what to exclude, what is important, and what is a minor detail that adds little to their analysis. But if such detail is important, if it is actually quite central to the analysis of an individual's personality and actions, what do you do then? One can, of course, use pseudonyms. This hides their identity, but this approach also would require one to disguise the names of the places and people with whom this individual interacted. One would also have to dispense with the use of any footnotes that could be used by others to discover the identity of the individual whose biography one was writing. This, however, can defeat a central tenet of historical research: that others be given the opportunity to verify or challenge the findings of the historian by retracing the historian's footsteps using the author's own bibliographical references. Taking this path has led a number of historians to simply eschew writing such biographies. There is another alternative, however. Historians could share their research findings with the slave owner's descendants and give them an opportunity to veto or allow the publication of the biography. This would allow the historian to respect the sensitivities of the communities, families, and individuals with whom he or she works. And if permission is granted, it would permit disclosure of slave origins when this is considered critical for understanding a person's thoughts and actions. Such an approach is standard procedure in the qualitative social sciences. Anthropologists are enjoined by both ethical standards and institutional review boards to "avoid harm to dignity and to bodily and material well-being," "to consider the potential impact of both their research and the communication or dissemination of the results of their work," "to obtain voluntary and informed consent." Historians are also encouraged to do the same.[15] This is the approach I take in this book. I discuss the slave origins of several individuals who figure prominently in the biographies presented here. And I include this information because it is central to my analysis of why certain persons responded to abolition as they did. But I have chosen to publish the actual names of only those individuals for whom I received permission from their descendants. Where no such permission was sought or received, pseudonyms have been used.

The felt stigma of slave origins is only one of the emotions identified in this study. Other feelings that shaped how slave owners responded to abolition include love, fraternity, anger, respect, loyalty. Discussion of such feelings is considered to be essential by many in biographical studies. Historian Robert Darton has noted that biography does a lot of things. It "eliminates the complications that weigh down accounts of entire societies, and it adheres to a narrative line that shows individuals in action. It . . . [gives] readers a sense of closeness to the men and women who shaped events." But perhaps more importantly, it "deals with motivations and emotions . . . it answers a voyeuristic desire to see through keyholes and into private lives."[16] Paula Backscheider also sees emotion as central to biographical writing. According to her, biography should allow the reader to see "through the subject's eye," "to feel exactly what hurt about each painful event." It should "touch the very soul, probe until the deepest, most shameful secrets and the most raw aches lie exposed."[17] It should include, in the words of Ira Bruce Nadel, "domestic privacies."[18] It is these concerns that inform these biographical sketches.

All of West Africa's slave owners were forced to respond to abolition. The outlawing of slavery was a clear attack on the status quo and an assault on their individual economic, social, and political interests. Responses, however, were varied. Some resisted abolition to their dying day. Others opted to adjust in ways they hoped would allow them to maintain their privileges. Still others actually embraced abolition. Why? What motivated them to take these different approaches? Were their actions motivated solely by their political and economic interests, or were they also influenced by their personal and intellectual trajectories?[19] And what legacies did their decisions leave for future generations? It is these questions that I address in the chapters that follow.

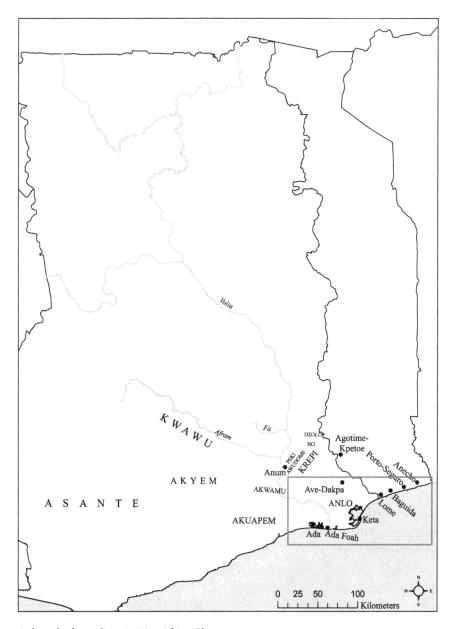

Anlo and other polities in West Africa/Ghana

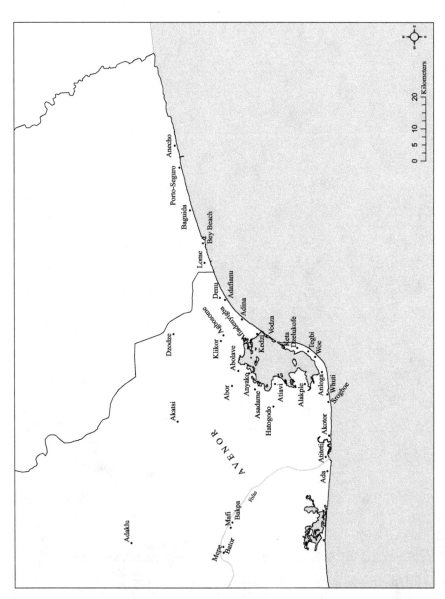

Towns significant in the lives of Amegashie Afkeu and Nyaho Tamakloe

1 Amegashie Afeku of Keta

Priest, Political Advisor, Businessman, Slave Owner

[There are] certain character traits I have observed in the Amegashie family, especially on the male side! My own grandfather and an uncle were also of the belligerent breed.

—William Sohne[1]

THIS STATEMENT BY William Sohne, a great-grandson of Amegashie Afeku, offers a particular perspective on the character of Amegashie Afeku. It is one that focuses on his legacy as a parent. According to Sohne, Amegashie demonstrated and passed down to some of his offspring such a high degree of assertive stubbornness that it could be quite off-putting.[2] Other perspectives about Amegashie come from documents written by German missionaries (who operated in the area in the late nineteenth century) when Amegashie was at the height of his reputation as priest, political advisor, businessman, and slave owner. They, too, found him very difficult, as did the British colonial officers who had the responsibility of overseeing the town of Keta where Amegashie lived and worked most of his life. Virtually everyone seems to agree, whether the assessment comes from the vantage point of a twenty-first-century descendant or from late nineteenth-century contemporaries. What did he do to deserve such a long-standing negative reputation?

Amegashie came of age in the mid-to-late nineteenth century when significant changes were occurring in West Africa. The establishment of Sierra Leone in 1787 and the British abolition of the slave trade in 1807 brought to the region a radically different understanding of the ethics and economics of the centuries-old institutions of slavery and the enslaved. These new understandings, championed largely by Europeans and Western-trained African missionaries,[3] challenged the notion that the West African export trade in human beings to the Americas was an unfortunate necessity, and that the mildness of slavery in Africa distinguished it from slavery in the West. Abolitionists promoted their ideas through word and deed, and forced others to at least listen to them because of their association with the British colonial government. West Africa's political and economic leaders (whose power rested in part on their large holdings of en-slaved women, men, and children) were not receptive to these new ideas. Most, in fact, were quite hostile. Slave masters voiced strong objections to the abolition of slavery. They protested to colonial officials, arguing that it would lead to their impoverishment. They worked with colonial administrators (many of whom had their own motives) to minimize the impact of the abolition on local communities. In time, most opted to adapt to the changed political circumstances. Many simply incorporated their slaves into their extended families. Others encouraged their slaves to redeem themselves so they could at least obtain minimal compensation for their losses. Still others actively resisted abolition.[4] Amegashie Afeku was among this last group. He, and others, moved their slaves into areas where European colonial authorities had not yet asserted their authority. They then demanded more labor while providing slaves with minimal food and time to work in their own fields. They even resorted to violence to prevent their slaves from leaving. Amegashie did all this. It is these actions that explain, in part, his reputation for being difficult.

In 1876, just two years after Britain abolished slavery on the Gold Coast, Amegashie was tried and convicted of ordering the capture and execution of two slaves (not even his own) who he thought were attempting to leave their masters to return to their original homes. Twice thereafter, in 1886 and 1889, he was again tried and convicted by the British colonial government, this time for slave dealing. Although he offered no explanation for his actions at these trials, his testimony indicates that he remained a firm believer in the institution of slavery and had no intention of accepting the moral arguments against the involuntary holding of human labor.[5] What led to his taking such a strong stance? Yes, his political, social and economic status was threatened by abolition. And, yes, he was clearly willing to use violence in support of his views. But what drove him to do so? Was it only a certain personality trait, as suggested by Sohne? Or was there something else? To what extent did he oppose British policies simply because they were part of the imposition of a larger imperial agenda? Or did his life experiences also contribute to his decision to strongly resist both abolition and colonial rule when so many others simply adjusted in ways that allowed them to maintain their political, economic, and social status? This chapter seeks to answer these questions. It does so by exploring the life of one individual, Amegashie Afeku, whose biography reveals a great deal about the motivations and emotions of others who took the same stance for their own reasons, but about whom we know so little.

Amegashie Afeku's Rise

Oral traditions and family histories indicate that Amegashie Afeku was born sometime in the early nineteenth century. Some say he was born and raised in

Keta. But others say, more plausibly, he was from Dzelukofe where his father and mother lived.

At the time of his birth, Keta was a fairly sleepy community. This was the case even though in previous decades it once hosted a diverse group of West Africans, Europeans, and Euro-African traders whose economic activities had long connected the area to the Atlantic world. In the late seventeenth century Keta was described as a thriving multi-cultural community where both Ewe, the local language, and Adangbe—spoken in the areas immediately west of the Volta River—was regularly heard.[6] In subsequent years, others from Akan-speaking communities and from towns and villages in the Anexo area east of Keta also settled in the district to govern or for purposes of trade and marriage. By the early eighteenth century Denmark claimed Keta and the surrounding coastline as its exclusive trading territory and in 1784, built a fort in the town, manned with both Danish and Danish African servants to defend its business interests. By the late eighteenth century, Keta was Denmark's third largest exporter of slaves on the Gold Coast and the upper Slave Coast. This trade, in turn, had encouraged greater economic activity within the Anlo polity as a whole (of which Keta was a part) and in Keta, in particular. Trade relations expanded to include significant economic relations between the Anlo villages and other towns on the Atlantic littoral as well as with distant villages in the interior. Opportunities for wealth accumulation within Keta grew accordingly. In 1803, however, Denmark officially abolished the slave trade. The result? Much of the economic activity in the town by the time of Amegashie Afeku's birth had shifted to Anlo towns west of Keta where slave traders could operate more freely out of the purview of the Danes. Trade in Keta did not cease totally, however. It simply declined. A lethal blow to the town's fortunes came in 1847. In that year, a dispute erupted between the Danish officers in the fort and some local residents over payment for the supplies the latter had sold to the Danes for the repair of their fort. Arguments led to a local boycott of the fort; negotiations broke down and violence erupted. Denmark then bombarded the town and destroyed it. Its residents fled.[7] Three years after the bombardment, in 1850, Denmark sold all its claimed possessions in West Africa—including the Keta fort—to Great Britain. The town's fortunes continued to languish, however, through 1852. At that time, there were still very few who had returned to Keta. In fact, those who lived in the town occupied just "four or five huts [that] stood beside the fort."[8] No one else was there. Even those occupants were not locals. Rather, they consisted of "a single British trader doing slow business in palm oil . . . and a few mulattoes," who had affiliated themselves with either the departed Danish or the current British occupants of the fort.[9]

In 1853, in an effort to reinvigorate the town economically, the British commandant of the fort, Thomas Evans, devised "a grand plan for the [largely empty locality]." He gave a group of Bremen-based German missionaries (the Nord-deutschen Missionsgesellschaft, NDMG) two blocks of the town for their own use.[10] In time, the town began to thrive again. In about 1855 the NDMG took control of a warehouse constructed by Commandant Evans to house stocks of European commodities and local produce. In 1857 J. C. Vietor, a merchant in Bremen affiliated with the mission, found the business opportunities created by the British presence in Keta to be so great that a ship he had sent to Brazil to engage in trade was able to load a cargo of goods at its stop in Keta sufficient in quantity that the ship dropped the Brazil leg of the trip and immediately returned to Bremen to sell their purchases. This, in turn, led Vietor to begin sending ships to Keta alone three times a year. Local merchants who had previously been selling their goods, whether slaves, palm oil, or cotton to buyers at other ports in the area, now began to send their agricultural produce—largely palm oil and some cotton—for sale to Keta. It was because of this increasing economic activity that Keta, slowly but surely, increased in population and became again a thriving trade town.[11]

As a resident of Dzelukofe and a trader himself, Amegashie must have been aware of these developments. This is probably what prompted him, in part, to move to Keta in 1859 after Keta's economic fortunes had begun to improve. On relocating to the town, Amegashie did not take long before contacting the seemingly prosperous missionaries. He approached them and demanded they recognize his right to a portion of the land that he claimed had been appropriated by the British and given to the mission. The land in question, according to Amegashie, contained his ancestors' remains.[12] By successfully persuading both the German missionaries and the British to recognize his claim, he was able to establish a base for himself in Keta.

During his early years in the town, Amegashie focused largely on religious matters. His grandfather, Togbi Lagbo, had been a priest associated with the Anlo war god, Nyigbla, but in his youth at Dzelukofe, Amegashie had not immediately followed in his grandfather's footsteps. Instead, he had begun trading in Ave-Dakpa, a town some fifty kilometers north of the Keta coast. It was in that town one day, while on a business trip, that he became ill. His sickness must have defied all attempts at a cure, for eventually his poor health was attributed to a god that was using the illness to call Amegashie to recognize its authority over his well-being. In such cases, an individual and/or his family would consult a diviner to determine which god was causing the illness. Once the deity was identified, that person—if healed after the diagnosis—was expected to become that god's devotee. According to family memory, Nyigbla was the deity that had caused Amegashie's illness. As the grandson of a Nyigbla priest, however, Amegashie became not just a worshipper of the god, but was inducted into the Nyigbla religious order as one of its priests.[13]

In moving to Keta, Amegashie maintained his interests in trade, but he also found the town to be an ideal location to establish a religious base, as indicated in the following German missionary report:

In about 1859 [Amegashie] settled in the near vicinity of the mission's farm. The first thing through which he drew attention to himself was that he claimed a piece of land that belonged to the mission because, as he stated, his ancestors were buried there. As it was only a small strip that bordered on his farm, and it was difficult at that time to get justice administered through the heathen national authority, his demand was granted. . . .[14]

He then launched into his activity as priest, which consisted of serving advice to all kinds of people who came from far and near with their different concerns. He set himself up as a rainmaker among other things. In those years, there was little rain, and the lagoon was completely dry.[15] There, he would assemble from time to time his followers, among whom were a number of elderly women. . . . One heard him at such assemblies often speaking loudly and calling his god, to which the women responded in chorus. . . .

One day [in 1860] it occurred to Amegashie to enact a law that no one may fire a gun during a certain time, as the shooting, in his opinion, held back the rain. His nearest neighbor, who at that time was the missionary Plessing . . . considered this law not to be binding on himself,[16] and at the next occasion he violated it. . . . Plessing happened upon a thief in the mission's garden, whom he scared off with a blast from his shotgun. . . . Amegashie came with great anger to the mission house and called Brother Plessing to account for his actions. A dispute arose during which the priest took a gun and hit the missionary with it, causing a wound which the latter had to plaster for a couple of weeks. . . . The fetish priest,[17] however, had not had enough. He returned to the missionary's yard in the afternoon with a gang, which tore down the freshly built walls; trampled upon the graves of departed missionaries when the loam was still wet; cut down beautiful palm and shade trees which the missionaries had painstakingly planted in the garden . . . filled in the well which the missionaries had dug in the yard and stole the hoist which [one of the missionaries] had carefully installed. This was still not enough. . . . The wild heathens then began to throw clumps of dirt and stones at our windows and to hammer and bang at them with their tools, making us believe that they were going to make their way in and raid our house. Thankfully, it never got that far. The windows and the doors withstood the attack and eventually the attackers slowly began to leave, letting silence fall over the missionary station. The old heathen was not a pleasant neighbor.[18]

This account dates and describes Amegashie's move to Keta. It also recounts the rather difficult relations that first developed between Amegashie and the missionaries. In time, however, he became one of the missionaries' greatest supporters.[19]

Amegashie's change of heart had everything to do with his ability to take advantage of the changing demographic and economic situation in Keta. By the 1860s, the Bremen Mission's economic success had encouraged other Europeans,

Euro-Africans, and African entrepreneurs to pour into the town.[20] The population swelled as did its prosperity. Amegashie and other local traders were able to purchase a wider range of goods from the many different European firms that had established themselves in the town. Still, fortunes from the sale of these commodities in the interior rose and fell. Many found themselves plunging deeply into debt when they were unable to find buyers.[21] Amegashie, however, was able to insulate himself from the vicissitudes of the market by persuading the political authorities in the Anlo capital of Anloga to allow him to act as their agent in Keta. He collected tolls from every European trader operating in the town including those associated with the Bremen Mission, and according to oral traditions, he kept quite a few of the proceeds for himself. In this way, by 1865 he was able to amass quite a fortune.[22] He married and supported six wives and fourteen children.[23] Over time, he was also able to acquire an undetermined but significant number of enslaved men, women, and children. These were all important symbols of wealth and status in nineteenth-century Anlo.

To solidify and maintain this status, Amegashie did even more. He made sure to connect himself through the marriage of his children to some of the most wealthy merchant families in Anlo society.[24] He also became a regular and active participant in the state council sessions that were held in the Anlo capital of Anloga. By 1871, in fact, some twelve years after he had moved to Keta, he had become both a confidant of the Anlo political and religious leader, the *awoamefia*, and a self-appointed enforcer of the hierarchical protocols that governed these sessions. When he thought certain individuals did not show enough respect for their superiors, he was not one to hold his tongue. In about May of 1871, for example, a missionary described what happened at one such state council session:

> The king [Awoamefia Letsa Gbagba] . . . wrapped himself in a piece of brown samite and came to the assembly, followed by Amegashi, the fetish priest and [chief] of Keta. They each had the priestly hat on their heads and a new pipe from Koeln [Cologne] in their mouths, from which they blew thick clouds of smoke. Amegashi announced the king and welcomed the assembly. Suddenly he saw John Tay, a native merchant, sit down on a chair. Amegashi now rose [and said]: "When the king of the land appears in an assembly, all must sit on the bare ground, even the elders. That is the law! Only he who is a king, all Europeans, people from Sierra Leone and those who have been baptized are excepted. They may sit on chairs. The one person [here] who has sat on a chair and who is not European, nor one of the Sierra Leone people, nor baptized, nor a king, he should have seated himself on the ground." John Tay refused. But then Amegashi began to alter his gestures, to rant and rave as though possessed, and John Tay had to leave to prevent it from escalating into a fight.[25]

Amegashie's focus on status influenced his own style of dress and comportment. In 1872 a Bremen missionary, G. B. Schiek, made the following observations.

Amegashie Afeku (seated). Courtesy of the Norddeutsche Mission.

[Amegashie] is [chief] and priest at the same time, but the latter [role] seems to recede more and more into the background. . . . He is a merchant and deals extensively in rum and palm oil which pass the lagoon in all directions. I declare: winning and trading are number one for him. The spirit of mammon has captured his heart. . . .

. . . He is an elderly man and seems not to see very much with his left eye. From time to time, he comes to the [Christian church] service, and as king, he dresses more beautifully than other people. A gown with golden dots that playfully [reflect] all colors—[a dress] he might have bought for a great deal of money from an Englishman—covers his not at all meager body. This is the way he appears on Sunday while passing through the streets of the sea-side town: a straw hat on his head, coral rings around his arm, holding imperiously in his right hand a long two-pointed but extremely crooked stick (which he sometimes paints red), and which has a straw cord tied to its point.[26]

In describing Amegashie, Schiek clearly reflected the Bremen Mission's emphasis on modesty in all things.[27] Still, it is likely that Amegashie relished his achievements. He insisted on hierarchical protocols in meetings of the Anlo State Council. He made sure to display his status when in public. He was a wealthy and respected merchant, and he demanded that others acknowledge this fact.

Amegashie, British Colonialism, and the Abolition of Slavery

In 1874, two years after Schiek penned his description of Keta's Nyigbla trader/ priest and the Anlo polity's fiscal agent in the town, Amegashie would face an unprecedented challenge to his wealth and authority. As mentioned, British colonial interest in the Anlo area officially began in 1850 when it bought Denmark's claimed possessions in West Africa, including the Keta fort. The British did more than simply assume control of Denmark's trade rights, however. Long concerned with the flow of firearms from coastal Anlo to the feared polity of Asante in the interior to the northwest, Britain claimed the right to rule Anlo. It extended the Gold Coast Colony to include Keta and the other Anlo villages that lay on the Atlantic littoral from the Volta River west of Keta, up to the town itself. It imposed the same poll tax it had enacted for the Gold Coast Colony. It outlawed the slave trade. Still smarting from the 1847 Danish bombardment of Keta, most Anlos were unwilling to militarily confront the British immediately. They were, however, prepared to resist in other ways. They refused to pay the poll tax. Only when threatened by Britain with yet another bombardment from the sea did they relent. In 1854 the Anlo launched yet another oppositional effort against the British presence when the political leadership in the Anlo capital of Anloga issued an injunction prohibiting all Anlo citizens from having any business with whites in the area, including those in Keta. No Anlo was to work for a European. No Anlo was to sell any commodities to them. Individuals caught defying the order were stopped and their goods confiscated. Threatened with starvation, the British soldiers in the fort simply went into town, took by force the food they needed from the women sellers as they were returning home, and arranged for payment later.[28] By 1856, however, the British withdrew from the town after finding that the profits from "legitimate" trade at Keta did not make continued occupation financially worthwhile. In 1874 they returned and extended to Keta their enforcement of the policies they had enacted in the Gold Coast Colony. These policies included bans on the importation of guns and the imposition of tariffs on a variety of goods, including liquor. Britain also used considerable violence against the local Anlo population to enforce these laws.[29]

Amegashie became a vehement opponent of British colonial rule. For not only did the British place heavy tariffs on a variety of trade goods he sold locally and in the interior, they also imposed a ban on the slave trade and outlawed slavery (enacted through a series of antislavery ordinances in 1874–75). From this date, slavery was officially abolished and one of the very terms by which many Anlos, including Amegashie, had come to measure their social status came under attack. Particularly threatening was the fact that, with abolition, the fort in Keta immediately became a refuge for those enslaved individuals who sought their freedom. Many slaves in Anlo had only recently been acquired. A particularly large group were Ewe-speakers like the Anlos, captured only three to five years earlier when Anlo participated with Asante in an invasion of the immediate interior. These captives knew that slavery had been abolished. They also knew where they came from. Many wanted to go home. Others had been purchased at the various slave markets in the area (at Ada, for example, on the Volta River) where large numbers of captives from what is now northern Ghana and Burkina Faso were sold. Buyers from Keta went regularly to these markets to purchase the labor they needed for household help or farm labor. Keta, however, was also where a number of African soldiers of northern origin, recruited from the ranks of the formerly enslaved, were posted. Their very presence prompted a number of their still-enslaved compatriots to seek their freedom at the fort.[30] Thus, slave owners in Keta, and in the other coastal towns where the British presence was felt, feared that the very terms by which they had operated in the world were seriously threatened. The British, however, did not want to undermine the output in "legitimate" trade goods (palm oil, cotton, and rubber) that was produced, in part, by the enslaved population, so they assured chiefs and slave owners that they would take no direct action in freeing the enslaved. Only those who came to them and could prove abuse would be allowed to obtain their freedom. Just as the British adjusted their enforcement of the antislavery ordinances to achieve their economic goals, so, too, did many slave owners. In Anlo, discussions of slave origins were banned. Euphemisms replaced the more blunt terms used to remind such individuals of their status. Families that had already been referring to their slaves as kin began to treat them more as equals rather than as subordinates over whom they could exercise absolute power.

Amegashie did not follow this course of action. He adamantly opposed the abolition. He refused to accept his slaves as anything other than property. Why? Answers can be found in his own history. Yes, he was a priest of Nyigbla, the Anlo's national war god, but he was a relatively minor figure in the order, one of many such priests affiliated with Nyigbla who were scattered throughout the Anlo polity. He held no high position within the order, nor did he have a particularly large number of religious followers. In addition, the worship of Nyigbla had been losing much of its popularity during this period to a new order, known as Yewe, that had recently entered the area.[31] Still, he was a wealthy and respected merchant. But he was also a descendant of a slave.[32]

His grandfather, Togbi Lagbo, a Nyigbla priest and trader in Keta before Amegashie assumed the same position, had married a woman by the name of Sekpui. This was Amegashie's maternal grandmother. She was from Agotime-Kpetoe, captured during a military conflict in the late eighteenth century and sold to Lagbo's brother. This brother then gifted Sekpui to Lagbo.[33] As an enslaved war captive, Sekpui's diminished social status would have certainly been well known to the residents of Keta, a status that would not have been enhanced

very much by her attachment to a Nyigbla priest. Sekpui gave birth to a daughter by the name of Ve. Once this girl reached the age of maturity, her father and
master, Togbi Lagbo, bequeathed her to one Sokpui of Dzelukofe. According to
Anlo oral traditions, before the relationship could be sexually consummated, Ve
was given to a Danish African officer posted at the fort in Keta. Traditions indicate that Ve had been admired by the officer when he saw her decorated and
paraded about the town as part of her marital ceremony.[34] Although we cannot
verify that the daughter of a slave would have been accorded such an honor, we do
know that the Anlo were very wary of European and Euro-African traders. In the
past, when some Anlos canoed out to waiting slave ships off the Keta coast, they
sometimes found themselves forcibly held and sold as slaves into the Atlantic
slave trade. The result was that most families in Anlo were deeply distrustful of
these traders. They came to be known in the local Ewe language as *yevuwo*, cun-
ning dogs. If a husband was interested in offering his intended wife to a European
or Euro-African trader for his personal comfort so as to reinforce his business
ties with that trader, virtually no family would have agreed to such an arrange-
ment for their daughter. They simply would not have trusted that trader not to
sell her into the slave trade. Ve, unfortunately, had no such family. Her mother
had been captured, enslaved, and transported to Anlo. She had been taken by
Togbi Lagbo without the consent of her parents. As a slave, she also would not
have been in a position to object to her own daughter, Ve, being used in this way.
So Ve went. She slept with the Danish African trader. She gave birth to three of
his children. Upon his death or departure from Keta, she resumed her relations
with Togbi Sokpui. It was at that point, in the early nineteenth century that she
gave birth to Amegashie Afeku.

If accounts from the mid to late nineteenth-century are correct, Amegashie
Afeku would have been subjected as a child to all manner of taunts about the
slave origins of his grandmother and mother. Most children who were ridiculed
in this way responded most often by withdrawing into themselves.[35] Even as a
young man in the early nineteenth century, Amegashie Afeku must have felt
keenly the stigma of his origins. Yet he managed to thrive. By ignoring the taunts,
by using the slurs to motivate himself, he developed a thriving business selling
a variety of imported commodities, liquor, tobacco, and cloth, to communities
in the interior. Once he became a Nyigbla priest and moved to Keta in 1859, he
used his business acumen and connections to those priests in his order who were
resident in the Anlo capital, and who also served as advisors to the Anlo political
leadership, to obtain even greater wealth.[36] Having reached the very heights of
power and influence in the Anlo hierarchy by 1871, just twelve years after having
moved to Keta, Amegashie embraced the status quo. When he felt threatened by
the increasing influence of such local Euro-African traders—so-called local "mulattoes" like John Tay, who operated as important and respected intermediaries

between the local political community and the early British colonial administration in Keta because of their command of the English language and yet their deep knowledge of local languages, customs, and culture—he made sure to put them in their place. Having worked diligently and against all odds to position himself among the wealthy and influential of Anlo, he was not about to allow any outsiders, the German missionaries or John Tay, to disrespect him or any of the other authorities who were at the political center of the Anlo polity. He let others know of his high status by using every opportunity to display his wealth. He invested in expensive smoking pipes from Europe and then flaunted them in public. He would appear regularly at different venues in Keta wearing ostentatious clothing to remind others of his position. He opposed the abolition and he was prepared to use violence to prevent its implementation.

Amegashie's stance would prove costly both to himself and to the enslaved. In 1876, two years after British forces reoccupied the Keta fort and began alerting the population that slavery was now abolished, a Bremen missionary couple, the Merzs, hired a group of porters in Keta to help them transport their goods to the inland missionary station at Waya. Among the porters were six men (accompanied by their wives and children) who had been captured by the Anlo during their participation in the 1869–71 Asante invasion of the interior. As reported by Merz, the men had been forced to work as slaves on the coast, but with the abolition they decided to return home. The roads in the interior were still quite unsafe, however, so travel was almost always by caravan. When Merz began organizing his trip to Waya, the six men and their families decided that this was their opportunity to return home. They offered their labor as porters to Merz. Their journey went well until they reached the village of Akatsi. There, on 29 January 1876, they were met by a group of men dispatched by Amegashie to prevent the former slaves from continuing further. The group of men, led by a man called Wa, had been instructed to force the former slaves to return even though, technically, they were free. They were not going to let the caravan proceed if it included the six men and their families. On their part, the formerly enslaved also resolved that they were not going to allow themselves to be re-enslaved. In the end, the confrontation turned violent as reported by Merz:

> In Akadi [Akatsi] . . . we wanted to get out of the midday heat. [But] just as soon as we were sitting under a tree, a staff-carrier came to me and gave me the staff in the name of the king, [or] so he said. I was frightened when I saw a cloth wound around the staff. . . . After several minutes, the well-known Wa came with a bunch of people armed to the teeth. We were surrounded and greeted. Wa assured me that he did not have anything against me. . . . [Rather,] it was explained that I had people with me that they [Wa's people] had stolen during the Asante time and who wanted to flee to their homes now. I explained that they were free under the law and had been given to me as free

[laborers]. We talked like this for three hours, back and forth. The [six] people begged me to protect them and to return with them to the coast. It was a terrible situation for me. My wife was there, who was naturally the person closest to me, but then there were also these black men and women, who cried for help and spoke of mercy and brotherly love. I talked until I could barely talk any more. . . . [Then] I saw that everything was made up. It wasn't the [Anlo] king who had sent them, but Amegashie from Keta. [The six men] assured me that they would be killed. They tried to be courageous and die peacefully, but [they also vowed] to defend themselves beforehand.

The [six men then] became increasingly angry. [They] told me to go away [and] they danced war dances and blew their horns. . . . I asked for my things to be taken to a courtyard and took my wife there. We had only been there a short time when the women came and asked for help. We couldn't do anything. At this point, one of the [ex-]slaves took a stick and delivered several strong blows to Wa's arm. I quickly grabbed my wife and said: now they will be killed. I immediately brought my wife into a hut, the door of which I broke down, and where other women had fled. . . . A second [former] slave came, who had had an ear and half of his face slashed away. We were sprayed with blood. This took place in a matter of minutes. I went back out into the courtyard with my wife. . . . I tried to break the fence, but it was impossible. . . . As soon as [the men outside the courtyard] saw that someone wanted to break through, they stuck their bayonets through the fence. One of the [former] slaves was next to the house with Wa and a few men to the side. Wa gave this man a neck wound at which point he fell to the ground. Spears were thrown from all sides. . . . The man whom Wa wounded jumped up again after receiving [yet] another blow and tried to give us his hand . . . his blood flew . . . all over . . . Finally they hit him to death with staffs.

At last we were able to break a hole in the fence, which I went through with my wife. In a hut further away, we listened to the rest of the fight. The men were killed.[37]

Even though the assault and murders occurred outside British jurisdiction, the colonial government heard about it and prosecuted Amegashie. They based their case not, however, on Merz's testimony, since he was unavailable at the time, having traveled back to Germany. Rather, they relied on the testimony of a number of Anlo witnesses who heard Amegashie give the order for the seizure of the former slaves.[38] Mind you, these were not Amegashie's people. He did not own them and had had nothing to do with them. It appears he acted largely to shore up the institution of slavery in Keta as a whole. By terrorizing those who sought to leave their masters and return home, Amegashie issued a warning to all those enslaved in Keta, including his own slaves, that he and others were prepared to use terror to uphold an institution that had been one of the markers of wealth and power in Anlo.

His conviction on murder charges (in absentia) in about 1876, however, changed nothing. Amegashie simply moved himself, his family, and all his slaves out of Keta to the village of Afiadenyigba, which was outside British control. He continued to regard his slaves as his property, and as far as he was concerned, he could do with them as he wished, no matter what the British government had to say. This endeared him neither to the British nor to his slaves. Two years later, in 1878, one of his "domestic servants" by the name of Quami, encouraged another of Amegashie's slaves to seek refuge at the fort.[39] In 1880 the British used their outstanding warrant for his arrest to prevent him from participating in a meeting of the Anlo chiefs that the British government had called.[40] Still he refused to relent. In that same year, he purchased at least one slave, a man by the name of Kwasi Moshi, who had been captured in what is now Burkina Faso and transported down the Volta River to be sold first at Ada and then again at Abolave, where he was purchased by Amegashie's agents. By 1885, when business on the Gold Coast began to suffer for all those, like Amegashie, who were involved in the import/export trade, he decided he could no longer ignore the British. He hired Gold Coast lawyer Edmund Bannerman to sue the colonial government over the confiscation of his land in Keta.[41] He asked for compensation for their use of his property to house a contingent of Fante policemen. He also appealed his conviction on murder charges. On all counts, Bannerman was successful. Amegashie was given title to the land and the conviction was overturned. He was now free to travel to Keta as he liked, without fear of arrest. Still, his attitude toward slavery did not change.[42]

In 1886, just one year after Bannerman's successes on his behalf, he was in court again, in person. He had been arrested at Afiadenyigba, brought to Keta, and charged with slave dealing, this time for selling Kwasi Moshi, whom he had bought in 1880, six years earlier. According to the testimony at the trial, Amegashie had entrusted Moshi with funds to conduct business on his behalf. When Kwasi lost money on the transaction, then failed to return immediately to his master at Afiadenyigba, Amegashie ordered him to be detained when he did return. He had Kwasi attached to a heavy log and held for two months. Thereafter, two of Amegashie's other slaves took Kwasi Moshi to Anexo to be sold so that the money from his sale could be used to cover the money he had lost. At Anexo they could find no buyer for him, so Amegashie's men took Kwasi Moshi to Dakpa, where Amegashie had long-established business ties. There, he was sold, but after staying four months with his new master, he escaped, traveled to Keta, and sought his freedom from the British at the fort in Keta. In his testimony, Amegashie argued that British law did not apply to the towns north of Keta and that he had acted mercifully toward Kwasi Moshi. He explained that he had bought Kwasi a wife and had provided him with a gun. He refused to acknowledge, however, that the men who had imprisoned Kwasi and then sold him did so on his own orders, since he as Kwasi's master would have ultimately been responsible for the debts that Kwasi incurred according to Anlo traditional law.

Amegashie denied culpability just as he had done when the government accused him of ordering the attack on the former slaves who had accompanied Merz. He denied involvement in Kwasi Moshi's sale even as he argued for the legitimacy of the institution of slavery beyond the borders of British territory.[43]

Convicted of slave dealing, Amegashie was fined twenty pounds, a substantial sum at that time. Still, he was undeterred. He was released after paying the fine. But in 1889 he was charged yet again for slave dealing based on the testimony of three of his slaves who had gone to the Keta fort in succession to seek their freedom. Again, he was arrested. Again, he was convicted and fined. This time, however, he offered no excuses. He said, "it is the custom in this country to purchase slaves to assist one." He refused to apologize for his behavior and then pleaded guilty.[44]

Why did Amegashie take this particular approach to the abolition of slavery when so many others in his community and elsewhere opted for a different approach, one that focused on adaptation rather than open and violent opposition? Why was he so committed to the old hierarchical order?[45] Part of the answer to this question can be found in his own background. As noted, Amegashie Afeku was a priest associated with one of the most powerful gods in Anlo, but he was of slave descent. Before his economic rise, he was merely a slave descendant attached to the powerful religious order. Over time, however, he was able to use his residence in Keta and the absence of any religious or political official from the Anlo capital to his advantage. He persuaded the authorities in Anloga to allow him to tax the Keta-based European traders on behalf of the polity. By taking advantage of the specific circumstances in which he found himself, he was able to acquire, on his own behalf, the wealth that became the basis for his influence in both Keta and Anloga. He took great pride in his achievements and made sure that others respected and acknowledged his authority. Yet he himself came from much humbler origins. He was the descendant of a war captive in a society that socially defined him as a slave descendant, "seven times lower in [terms of] respect than a free person."[46] But it was also this same social and political order that had given him the opportunity to reach the heights of power. This explains, at least in part, his fierce defense of the old hierarchical order and his absolute refusal to adjust to the changed political and social landscape created by British colonialism.

Documenting the history of such an individual, describing the details of his life and times, tells us a great deal about slavery in Africa and the concerns that led many to not just resist and then adapt, but to resolutely defy both colonial rule and the abolition up to their dying days. This biographical sketch reveals the complex and peculiar circumstances that allowed Amegashie Afeku to move from slave descendant to slave owner, to embrace both the German missionary presence as well as the old Anlo hierarchical order, to welcome the business generated by the European presence at Keta, but to abhor and to actively fight against European colonial rule and the abolition of slavery. I offer a portrait of a slave owners that humanizes him, but also horrifies as we see the actions he was prepared to take to preserve the life he had come to cherish and hold dear.

How unusual was Amegashie? In his use of violence, he was far from unique. Others did the same. In 1875, just one year after the British colonial government had abolished slavery in the Gold Coast Colony, a group of slave owners in the interior of the colony hired some men to capture and return to them those male slaves who were making their way to the coast to freedom by working as hammock bearers. Their efforts proved unsuccessful, but the enslaved men suffered severe beatings at the hands of the slave catchers.[47] In 1896, in Amegashie's own community of Anlo, a woman slave owner ordered the capture and killing of one of her female slaves when she attempted to free herself, her prepubescent daughter, and her infant child by returning to her hometown in the interior.[48] In 1908 and 1910, just a few years after France's abolition of slavery in their West African territories began to be enforced, someone, presumably some slave owners in the Timbuktu district of northern Mali, ordered the killing of a grandmother and a mother, while another mother was "brutally tortured." Their "crimes"? They had attempted to reclaim their children from the children's owners.[49] In 1910, near the town of Kita (in what is now southern Mali), some masters attacked a group of enslaved women, men, and children seeking to leave the area.[50] This kind of violence continued in this region as late as the 1950s. In a 2005 conversation with historian Jeremy Berndt, the imam of Seke (a small town in northern Mali) "recalled how, during his boyhood in the 1950s, the villages' masters would band together to administer beatings to a disobedient slave."[51]

Amegashie was certainly not alone, in Anlo or in West Africa, in his use of violence to defend what he considered his right to buy, sell, and own slaves. He was also not unique in his ability to move from slave descendant to politically influential and wealthy slave owner. We know of individuals in other parts of West Africa who were able to do the same, although such individuals were far from the norm.[52] This biography of Amegashie allows us to go beyond the listing of violent incidents perpetuated by slave owners. Instead, we have a portrait of an individual who was able to take advantage of the opportunities that came his way. He did so despite his status as a slave descendant, and perhaps was so successful because he had so much to prove, both to himself and to others. He was stubborn to the point of using violence to gain and retain what he wanted. A staunch opponent of colonial rule, Amegashie also refused to accept the notion that slavery was unethical and now illegal. His life illustrates not only the nature of slavery in West Africa, but also the very human struggles that took place with the imposition of colonial rule.[53]

Legacies

By the time Amegashie Afeku died in 1895, he had achieved a great deal. He had risen from slave descendant to a position of respect and influence within the Anlo political system and had successfully used that position to enhance his economic standing. He fought off imprisonment for slave dealing even though the British presence in Keta meant that he lost those who wanted to be free of his control. Many more of his slaves remained with him in Afiadenyigba. They farmed; they married; they had children. And for a period, as noted by one of his descendants, whom I shall call Togbi Dza, they remained as slaves.

> [Our founding elder] had a ranch. . . . After the abolition of slavery, he sent all his slaves there to work on the farm. They worked, gave the lion's share of the fruits to the master, keeping some for themselves. They would marry amongst themselves, have children and stay on to work. They could never claim the land for themselves; they were slaves, laborers and just worked for their master.

It was only after his death that changes took place. Amegashie's former slaves and their descendants became members of the larger Amegashie family. They gained the right to retain the fruits of their labor. They managed the land on which they had worked for generations as they saw fit. These changes, however, have not erased all distinctions, as is evident in another of Togbi Dza's statements:

> The descendants [of Amegashie's slaves] are still on the land tilling it and by right I should receive some payment, . . . but now they claim to be part of the . . . family with all rights. So I can't sack them.[54]

At least for Togbi Dza, the descendants of Amegashie's slaves are different from the rest of the family; they are subordinate members, less than the equals of those who are Amegashie's direct descendants. These differences, it would appear, have also been policed. Marital unions are said to have occurred only within the slave community. None of Amegashie's own direct descendants are said to have intermarried with those of slave descent. Implied as well is the notion that only because the formerly enslaved are now defined as family (a development that may have been beneficial in the past when large families were important for political and economic reasons, but which is no longer so critical) have they escaped the possibility of being moved off the land. As a descendant of Amegashie, Togbi Dza may be unusual. His views may be quite unrepresentative of those held by other family members. What is important about his comments, however, is the fact that they are not unusual either in Ghana or in West Africa.

This kind of remembering, normally discussed only in hushed tones or confined to the meetings called by family elders, can become quite public. In 1995, this intimate aspect of Ghana family politics burst onto the public stage.[55] The occasion was a court case. A branch of the royal family in Asante-Mampong in south-central Ghana had selected and installed their candidate, Nana Akuamoah Boaten Ababio, as the next paramount chief of the polity. They found themselves challenged, however, by another branch of the family. The challengers claimed that Nana Ababio was ineligible to hold the position because he was of slave descent. After much litigation the case ended before the Ghana Supreme Court. Its ruling was stunning to many.

> The Supreme Court of the Republic of Ghana stripped Nana Akuamoah Boaten Ababio, "a highly educated [businessperson] and respected gentleman" of a quite prominent and important chieftaincy position. It did so because he was of slave origins. The court based its ruling on the fact that "customary laws and usages" which barred slave descendants from such positions were recognized as part of the legal code of Ghana in the country's 1992 constitution. In issuing the judgment, the chief justice noted that discrimination by family heads against those members of the same family who were of slave descent "was not repugnant to justice, equity and good conscience." In other words, while the 1874 Abolition of Slavery Ordinance, the 1874 Emancipation of Persons Held in Slavery, and the 1930 Reaffirmation of the Abolition of Slavery Ordinance "pronounced freedom for slaves in the Gold Coast [i.e., Ghana], they did not . . . protect their rights to property," in this case access to a traditional political office. Nana Akuamoah Boaten Ababio was removed from office. His slave status barred him from holding such a position. He was informed in no uncertain terms that he had no right of access to the property of the family of which he and the descendants of his ancestor had been a part for generations.[56]

This kind of ruling is not unique. In 2006, a similar case was heard in Niger's court system in 2006 in which slavery was upheld because that country also recognized customary laws that made certain forms of slavery legal.[57]

In other places in West Africa, the hierarchical order is upheld by local beliefs and social norms. In northern Mali, for example, the descendants of former slave masters—like many others in West Africa—have been unable to maintain their economic superiority or political authority over those whom they once controlled. Opportunities created during the colonial and postcolonial periods, and, in the case of Mali, the devastating drought that hit the country in the early 1970s and early 1980s, generated a set of conditions that allowed some formerly enslaved to shed their dependency on their former masters.[58] Yet, many former slave owners retain a strong sense of superiority. According to Baz Lecocq, these attitudes—found among the Tuareg peoples of Mali—are grounded in ideas about the innate differences that exist between the formerly enslaved and free persons. Many free people "see the mind frames of free and slave as naturally given and not as cultural constructs. Both free persons and slaves have intelligence, but of a different nature." These innate differences are said to be evident in how the two are perceived. According to this belief system, "a free or noble person knows shame and honour, which restrains his or her conduct. Slaves, by contrast, do not know shame or honour and behave, by nature, in an unrestrained way. This becomes apparent in a person's bearing, for example, in the way in which one dances or sits. Free persons dance rather stiffly and slowly, while slaves dance unrestrainedly with more movements. Slaves, male and female, sit on their heels (a shameless posture as it is associated with defecation), whereas free men proudly sit upright and cross-legged, and free women lie elegantly on their sides. . . . Slaves are [also] unable to understand religious duties, (being by nature thievish and deceitful)."[59] Even if, as has happened, many people of slave descent now carry themselves differently and hold high official positions in their communities because they took advantage of educational opportunities long shunned by free Tuareg, these individuals are "still seen as 'slaves' without any prestige or status outside their personal achievements and qualities."[60] Similar ideological hierarchies exist in northern Benin, Niger, Mauretania, and central Mali, although they are being renegotiated and challenged.[61]

Current studies indicate that Ghana does not follow this pattern. There are no widely held notions on the part of the descendants of former slave owners that they are inherently superior to the descendants of the formerly enslaved. They have no interest, collectively, in upholding community-wide, age-old hierarchies. This is not to say, however, that slave descent is totally irrelevant. It remains a stigma, to be discussed largely in private. That such origins are at times revealed publicly, contrary to social norms, as happened in the 1995 case before the Ghana Supreme Court, is unusual. Yet this case reveals a hidden reality. Some still find it difficult to accept the full consequences of the abolition of slavery. For them, distinctions must be made, if only at the family level. This is the legacy Amegashie (and others who were similarly adamantly opposed to abolition) bequeathed to West Africa. Not all embraced this legacy. Many have rejected it. But it is a legacy that continues to linger in the heads and hearts of some.

2 Nyaho Tamakloe of Anlo

Of Chieftaincy and Slavery,
of Politics and the Personal

The pig may make the water on the surface of the pond ripple, but not the sea;
the frog may go hunting in the pond but not in the ocean; the hippopotamus
flips normal boats over, but not the heavily-laden sand boat.

The old tortoise in the pond says she can compete with a giant snake. If the
snake doubts her power, then the snake should just try to devour her.

—Katechist Elias Tamakloe[1]

THESE PRAISE POEMS, composed in the late nineteenth century, were offered
in honor of just one person: Nyaho Tamakloe of Anlo. He was the sea that no
pig could disturb; the ocean that would overwhelm any hunter; the sand-boat
that could nullify the power of the hippo. Not even the strongest of enemies (the
snake) could match the power of the old tortoise (Tamakloe). He was wealthy, a
highly respected military leader, a patriarch who headed a household with numerous wives, and the owner of many slaves. This is how he is remembered in
word and song today.

But who was Tamakloe really? These praise poems emphasize his military
prowess. He participated in every major conflict (five in all) that the Anlo army
engaged in from 1865 to 1869. In many, he personally led his troops into battle.
Yet he was so much more than this. In many ways, he was an enigma. He fought
against the British three times in the mid to late nineteenth century, but when the
Anlo were finally defeated and brought under colonial rule, Tamakloe embraced
the British presence. He was illiterate but used his great wealth to invest in land,
mining enterprises, and the education of the most promising students from his
extended family. He believed in and was a major sponsor of the local polytheistic
religious orders that operated in Anlo, yet he strongly supported the establishment of a number of different Christian churches and schools in the area. One
has to wonder, who indeed was this Tamakloe?

Of greatest interest in this brief biographical sketch is his approach to slavery
in the age of abolition. Tamakloe, who owned many slaves himself, became by the

CAPT. NYAHO TAMAKLOE I,
(Chief of Wuti/Anlo),
Left Wing Divisional Chief of Anlo, Died on 18th
March, 1918.

Nyaho Tamakloe. Courtesy of the author.

1890s (in the last thirty years of his long life)[2] a major figure in the fight to end the stigma associated with slave descent. He sent not just one or two of his formerly enslaved dependents to the missionary-run schools in the area, but provided the opportunity for all under his authority, both free and formerly enslaved, more than a hundred boys and girls, to obtain a Western education that was also free of charge. He elevated a number of his former slaves to the status of *hanuwo*, village leaders, essentially placing them on par with the other village leaders and chiefs in Anlo who were of free descent. Unusual for his many accomplishments in the business of war and moneymaking, he was extraordinary on the issue of slavery. To date, we know of no other slave owner in Anlo, in the Gold Coast or in West Africa who managed his slaves' transition from slavery to freedom as he did.

Many in Anlo and, for that matter, elsewhere in West Africa, as noted, resisted the 1874 slave abolition laws imposed on them by the British. They wrote petitions to express their dismay. Others, like Amegashie, used violence to intimidate the enslaved men, women, and children into submission to their will. The vast majority reluctantly adjusted. They began recognizing their former slaves as independent members of their families and communities. They banned the use of abusive language, even as they maintained hidden transcripts about the origins of such individuals.[3] This was the path of least resistance. Colonial policies abolished slavery, but did little to encourage masters or slaves to alter the bonds that defined the institution. Individuals still valued large families as a source of economic, social, and political power. Recognizing the formerly enslaved as independent, yet junior branches of one's lineage allowed unspoken hierarchies to remain in place. Why, then, should anyone who owned slaves embrace a more egalitarian ethic when social hierarchies and family ties could remain intact despite abolition? Yet this is precisely what Tamakloe did. Why? To answer this question, I explore the life of Nyaho Tamakloe of Anlo. How did he understand and respond to the changing world in which he lived? How did he react to the shifting political, economic, and social dynamics that characterized the late nineteenth and early twentieth century? What prompted him to challenge his society in how they had traditionally positioned the enslaved? Answers to these questions can tell us a great deal about how both political, social, and economic concerns, as well as personal experiences shaped the decisions of traditional leaders in the age of abolition in West Africa.

Tamakloe as Military Leader

Born in what was likely the 1830s in the small Anlo community of Whuti, we know little about Tamakloe's early years. Family oral histories trace his genealogy and little else. We know virtually nothing of his parents or siblings except their names; we know little of his childhood or adolescence. Rather, Tamakloe emerges in the memories of local historians only through his military achievements in a series of wars that had their origins in times long before his birth. In the eighteenth and early nineteenth centuries, Anlo was a significant military power in the lower Volta River region. It regularly waged war to gain control over a set of saltworks at Ada, to expand its dominance over trade at the mouth of the river, and to maintain trade contacts with its economic allies in Asante and Akwamu. On average, Anlo waged war every nine years as indicated below:

Year	Name of Conflict	Major Opponent(s)
1750	Nonobe war (1750)	Agave and Ada
1769	Ada war	Ada
1770	Ada war	Ada
1784	Sagadre war	Ada, Anexo
1785	Keta-Anlo war	Keta
1792	War with Danes	Danish traders in Keta
1830	Peki war	Peki
1833	Peki/Awudome war	Peki

By the early to mid-nineteenth century, however, the Anlo focus on military assertiveness was beginning to be tested as a result of other developments.

The 1807 abolition of slave trade on the Gold Coast prompted, by the 1830s, a number of Euro-Africans, Brazilians, and Spaniards to move to Anlo to take advantage of the opportunities to engage in the slave trade which was being suppressed elsewhere on the coast. They brought with them the kinds of financial assets and commercial networks that were largely unknown in the area at that time. Anlo had never been a major site for the export of enslaved men, women, and children. This changed in the 1830s. Money flowed into the polity. The connections that the Euro-Africans, Brazilians, and Spaniards brought with them opened up previously unavailable outlets for local entrepreneurs to engage in the trade. Sleepy hamlets and villages like Woe and Atorkor became larger slave entrepôts, and Anlo citizens who had been relatively unknown achieved wealth and fame. This, in turn, generated deeper transformations. Those who had previously been defined as the most powerful and prestigious in their communities were gradually being challenged to share the spotlight with others. Where once military prowess, ownership of powerful gods, and membership in the community's founding families had structured the local political and social hierarchy, wealth was added to this mix. Money allowed the Euro-Africans, in particular, to entrench themselves at the highest levels of Anlo society. They paid to obtain membership in the most respected clans in the community. They offered money in exchange for the use of Anlo's military services in their own trade disputes, and they introduced new gods into the community to bolster the Anlos' confidence in their ability to win in battle without suffering major losses.[4] Tamakloe witnessed none of this. He had not even been born yet. But during his formative years, in the 1850s and '60s, this mix of status based on performance in war, ownership of powerful gods, and the ability to take advantage of changing circumstances to become wealthy structured the way he chose to pursue his own path to high social status within his community.

The first set of opportunities for Tamakloe to make a name for himself came in the 1860s. The medium was war. Within a space of eight years, Anlo militarily engaged its enemies six times. Tamakloe participated in every one, first as a combatant, and then, beginning in 1869, as *miafiaga*, commander of the left wing of the Anlo military.[5]

Year	Name of Conflict	Major Opponent(s)
1865	Funu war/Atiteti war	Ada and British forces
1866	Second Agoue war	Agoue and British forces
1867	Adidome war	Ada and British forces
1868	Datsutagba war	Ada and British forces
1869	Agotime war	Ho and Agotime forces
1873	Glover war	Ada and British forces

These conflicts, however, were different from the ones waged before. Prior to the 1860s, the wars in which Anlo found itself were largely local disputes,[6] waged to determine who would control certain fishing grounds and salt ponds as well as the trade routes around the mouth of the Volta River. By the 1860s Britain had entered the picture to pursue its own interests in the region. These interests involved putting an end to the Atlantic slave trade that had been booming in Anlo since the 1830s, encouraging commerce in "legitimate" goods, and ending the many disputes that were disrupting commerce around the Volta River. To achieve these goals, Britain was prepared to resort to military force. In 1865, 1866, and 1873, it did just that. The result: Anlo suffered great losses and was forced to recognize its inability to face successfully a more powerful enemy. In two of the conflicts, the Funu/Atiteti, and the second Agoue war, Britain deployed its navy off the coast and made it clear that they had both the ability and willingness to use their ships' armaments to bombard and destroy every Anlo coastal town and village within the range of their guns. In the third conflict, the Glover war, British forces launched an invasion of the polity from the north, which if carried to its fullest extent, would have forced the Anlo to flee to the very Atlantic coastline where military ships awaited to bombard them from the sea.[7] For Anlo, this was a most sobering revelation. Britain, moreover, was not the only superior military force it confronted in the 1860s and '70s. In the 1869–71 war, Anlo faced the state of Asante, not as an enemy, however, but ostensibly as an ally. In this war, known in Anlo as the Agotime war, Asante, Akwamu, and Anlo joined forces to invade the interior polities in the region known as Krepi. Their goal was to bring the many independent polities in the region under control so that Asante and Akwamu forces could better control for their own benefit the political and economic activities in that region. The war did not go well for the three allies, however. They found it impossible to combat successfully the guerilla tactics employed by their Krepi enemies. So when the Asante forces, the most numerous and powerful of the three, found themselves bogged down in a war that yielded far too little booty that they could display on their return home as symbols of their success, they turned on the few allies they had in the interior and enslaved them. They then threatened to attack Anlo. This was an invasion that the Anlo knew they would not be able to repel.[8] These experiences, and the fact that they suffered quite heavy losses in all the wars they waged between 1866 and 1873, forced Anlo's political leaders to reassess the approach they had traditionally taken to defend their economic interests. For Tamakloe, this reassessment was especially necessary given his own experiences in these wars.

According to family and friends, Tamakloe lost his brother, Kwasi, in the Agoue conflict.[9] No account of this war mentions his participation without also noting that he lost this brother. The same is true of his participation in the Agotime war. In that conflict he lost his nephew. Such oral recollections may signal the importance of letting listeners know that prominent individuals suffered personal losses like others in the community. But it could also indicate how deeply Tamakloe himself felt these losses. Similar experiences certainly influenced the thinking of other Anlo military commanders. In 1847, when an Anlo citizen was killed by a Danish officer resident in Keta in a dispute that erupted into violence over the quality of firewood delivered to the Danish occupied fort, the supplier of the wood, Dzokoto of Anyako, who was then the *miafiaga*, left-wing commander of the Anlo army, was so distressed over the death that he asked his people to "give him a mat so that he may lie down and die for he had caused the whole thing."[10] In 1860, when the Anlo first fought in the eastern coastal polity of Agoue, the loss of life was so great that the commander of the entire Anlo army, the *awadada*, Axolu felt such personal disgrace that he refused to return to Anlo. He preferred to remain in exile. Six years later, when the Anlo decided at the urging of Axolu's nephew to send an army to him in exile that he would lead yet again in another war in Agoue, their losses were again so extensive that Axolu resolved never to return to Anlo. The shame was too great.[11]

Tamakloe, who succeeded Dzokoto in 1869 as *miafiaga*, would have also probably despaired over the heavy loss of life that occurred when he, too, was in command.[12] Whether or not Tamakloe responded to these losses by following in the footsteps of Dzokoto or Axolu, we cannot know. We have no evidence one way or the other. We only know that his performance as both a combatant and later as military leader won him much praise. He was the sea that no pig could disturb; the ocean that would overwhelm any hunter; the sand-boat that could nullify the power of the hippo. But Tamakloe was also deeply and personally affected by

the entire experience. Not only did he lose many of his troops, but he also suffered the loss of relatives with whom he was very close. Thus, it was after taking
a battering as a commanding officer in the Agotime and Glover conflicts, and after realizing his inability to militarily resist the superior forces of Britain and
Asante, that Tamakloe worked with many of the other Anlo chiefs to pursue a
different path. They decided to abandon the use of military force to protect their
economic interests, and they pursued, instead, peaceful engagement with the
world of commerce. For Tamakloe, this meant throwing himself into the work
of trading, export agricultural production, and investment with as much energy
as he had attacked the enemy in war. Local oral histories indicate that Tamakloe
energized his troops during the Glover war by insisting that "No animal that
visits a farm should return with [even] its feet (*La ve boto metsoa afo yiaweo*)." He
employed this same approach in pursuing his economic interests.[13]

Tamakloe as Businessman

To achieve his goal of financial success, Tamakloe worked closely with various
trading firms in the area. These included G. B. Williams, F. A Swanzy, and Vietor
and Sons. It was from these businesses that he obtained the various commodities
that were in demand locally and in the interior. He employed the slaves he captured in war and bought in local markets in the marketing of these goods, and in
producing copra, the principal agricultural crop in demand on the international
market that could be grown in the Anlo area. He sponsored the establishment
of three different Yewe religious orders (one each in Whuti, Keta, and Dzelukofe), all of which embraced the notion that religious influence was not incom-
patible with commerce. He then—like other Yewe owners—used these groups
to enhance his own reputation—already well established because of his military
career—by gaining their political and economic support. He invested heavily in
land, buildings, and other economic opportunities in which some of the Yewe
members would work.[14]

A list of his known investments shows that Tamakloe was particularly interested in positioning himself to work in Keta, which had become the most important center of trade after the British occupied the town in 1874. He bought
several plots of land and existing buildings, which he then leased to merchant
firms and the Hausa immigrant community. Aware that British efforts to control the importation of guns, gunpowder, and liquor through the imposition of
various duties had spawned some very lucrative opportunities for smuggling,
he established stores in Denu and Asadame, which were outside British control
at the time. More significantly, Tamakloe did not confine his business interests
to the immediate Anlo area. Instead, he used his contacts to invest in mining
operations, timber harvesting, cattle ranching, and agricultural projects in the
neighboring regions of Avenor and Klikor, and as far away as Akyem, about two

hundred forty kilometers to the northwest, and in Baguida, about fifty kilometers from Keta in what is now the Republic of Togo.[15]

Preliminary List of Nyaho Tamakloe's Business Dealings[16]

Date	Business Transactions/Financial Dealings
1879	Bought by this date his first properties in Keta (occupied by the British colonial government) and Denu (outside British jurisdiction where duty-free liquor and gunpowder could be imported).
1882	Bought Keta Lagoon side house and land from Theophelus Campbell.
c. 1883	Opened business operations in Lome.
1884	Owned a rum shop at Sadame, near Anyako by this date.
	Received £140 as a government-recognized chief for four years of unpaid stipends, and £35 annually thereafter.
	Bought for £5 a large area where the Catholic Mission would later be built.
	The seller subsequently thought he had been cheated and refused to repay a loan of £5 from Tamakloe because he thought he had been duped into selling land for too little. Tamakloe was reluctant, but in 1884 agreed to write off the £5 loan as part of the price of the land.
1885	Bought from two Vodza residents a large property in Keta/Hausa town.
	Leased this land for nineteen shillings a month for ten years in 1904.
	Bought from two Dzelukofe men land in Keta on the ocean side for 16 shillings, six pence.
1887	Sued successfully the British government for damages to his property in Whuti for the sum of £500.
	Ordered £235 worth of goods (rum, gun powder, guns, indigo blue yarn, cartridges) from G. B Williams.
1890	Granted land to the Catholic Mission, 9 June.
1891	Purchased land in Keta from a Dzelukofe landowner.
	Granted land in Klikor by chiefs there and by Awoamefia Amedor Kpegla "in love, good will and affection [for] their friend." In recognition of this gift, Tamakloe gave to the chiefs: thirty-six heads of cowries, six demijohns of rum, twenty pieces of cloth, forty heads of tobacco. This land was later developed into a coconut plantation for the export of copra.
1898	Bought land in Keta from the Tay Agozo family through his son. E. N. Tamakloe.
1902	Bought land from George Briggance Williams of Freetown (resident in Keta) for £75.
	Bought a one-twentieth share in a land concession in Akyem (held by Thomas Wulff Cochrane of Accra) for purposes of mining, timber extraction, farming, or fishing for £25 on 15 March.

	Paid £69 for the purchase of a half share in a land concession in Kwawu held by Thomas Wulff Cochrane of Accra.
1906	Bought property in Keta from Anyidoho, who had acquired it after loans were not repaid.
1907	Rented a building to the commercial firm Bodecker and Meyer of Keta for £2 a month for 10 years.
1908	Successfully sued in the Gold Coast Supreme Court to be declared owner of Tetu Creek and Hillock.
1909	Purchased property in the Dekpo Avenor district for agricultural production for £9.
	Ended the lease to the immigrant Hausa community in Keta that had been paying 1 shilling per house on between four hundred and five hundred houses to reside on his land.

Perhaps the most remarkable aspect of this phase in Tamakloe's life is that he pursued all these investment opportunities without being able to read or write. Literacy had become necessary to take maximum advantage of the economic opportunities brought about by the end of the Atlantic slave trade, but as an illiterate, he was undeterred. He sought and received the support of Western-educated members of his community. Throughout the 1880s and '90s, Tamakloe worked especially closely with Paul Sands—a Euro-African born and raised in Keta—who "[wrote] all his documents and necessary papers." This connection and his ties to other Euro-African families (the Malms and the Williams), allowed him to benefit from their social and economic connections, as well as their knowledge of how best to navigate the world of British colonialism while his own sons received the education they needed to assist their father in future years.[17]

In addition to educating many of his own children, Tamakloe also supported the expansion of Western educational opportunities for the larger community. In 1882, when Tamakloe's secretary, Paul Sands, opened a school for local youth to learn English (the language of business) at a younger age than that provided by the German missionaries who had worked in the area since 1853, it was Tamakloe who provided the school with its first building and then enrolled four of his sons.[18] In 1898 he donated land in Keta to the Catholic Mission, which, like Sands's school, taught English at a much earlier age than the Bremen Mission schools.[19] Of interest here is the fact that, when Tamakloe made the grant of land to the Catholic Church, he requested and was granted as compensation for his generosity the right for his many children to attend the school free of charge. No boy or girl from his massive, extended family had to pay school fees.[20]

Tamakloe's request is indicative of the value he placed on Western education—and especially education in the English language—at a time when colonialism had become an unavoidable reality, and English the language of business. But it is also significant for another reason. He made no distinction among the children in his household based on their social origins. As remembered by an Anlo elder, "that is how the family got so large. When [the Catholic priests] said those with Tamakloe wouldn't pay school fees, some of my friends [from Adjato, one of his slave villages] changed their names to Tamakloe and . . . became Tamakloe overnight."[21] Equally important, Tamakloe didn't object to this development. In fact, he probably approved of it. For in offering this opportunity to obtain a Western education—and one that was free of charge no less—Tamakloe must have seen in the actions of those who took advantage of this—more than one hundred boys and girls, both free and formerly enslaved—an echo of the approach he had taken himself to achieve both fame and wealth. In war and in business, Tamakloe had allowed no opportunity to escape his net. By taking advantage of Tamakloe's deal with the Catholic Church, so, too, were his dependents (his children and their parents). That he made this opportunity available at all says a great deal about Tamakloe. Times were changing. He, like most Anlo leaders, had to adjust, and most did. But Tamakloe did more than adjust. He was determined to take maximum benefit of the opportunities that these changes brought. And he was not going to be deterred by preexisting social norms.

Prior to the 1874 colonial abolition of slavery, enslaved labor was at the heart of the hierarchical system that characterized Anlo social, political, and economic life. The number of slaves one had was an indicator of one's wealth, a number that wealthy individuals frequently displayed publicly through the outdooring of wealth stools (*hozikpui*) in which the number of slaves one owned was represented by the number of cowries strung around the stool's central pillar. Slaves and other household members (free wives, descendants, and servants) produced, processed, bought, and marketed the goods that formed the financial foundation of the wealthy. A large household of both enslaved and free also constituted a base of constituents that the wealthy could use to reinforce their political influence. According to oral histories, Tamakloe was deeply involved in this long-standing institution. In addition to those whom he captured in war, he is said to have "accepted slaves [as repayment for debts]. . . .[22]

If the ownership of slaves brought praise and power to the wealthy, no such acclaim was accorded to those without. The enslaved and the poor were viewed with considerable disdain. This was especially evident prior to 1874. In 1853, when European missionaries from Germany first began working in the area, they opened schools and used them to introduce young people to Christianity. Few locals were prepared to send their children for instruction, however. They had no interest in this new religion and they were not prepared to part with their children at a time when the demand for enslaved children, both in domestic markets and for export to the Americas, was still quite high. Parents who did send their children to the missionaries were frequently ridiculed and scorned in public.

They were accused of selling their children because they were hungry and had no other means of financial or social support.[23] The children themselves were also taunted. As noted by a German missionary in 1875, "the mere mention of the term '*ame fe fle*,' bought person, makes slave children pull back. They sink . . . into quiet brooding for they cannot change their situation."[24]

Only after 1874, when the British abolished slavery, did the Anlo pass laws that banned the practice of referring to others as slaves. The new regulation was in response to fears that if locals continued to abuse the formerly enslaved by reminding them of their low social status, those who knew where they came from could and would leave to return home. This would destroy the "wealth-in-people" that many families had accumulated over the decades."[25] Changes also occurred in inheritance practices. Former slave masters began to bequeath to the children of their formerly enslaved wives, significant inheritances because the children of these wives had no maternal relatives from whom they could obtain the material assistance they would need to establish themselves as economically independent individuals in the community. Slave owners who did this had to face the wrath of their free wives, but in defying these objections they could reference the fact that local ethical concerns, found in Anlo proverbs, also expressed sympathy for the enslaved.

Anlo-Ewe Proverbs[26]
A slave that has twins has a lot of work (for she has no one to help her).

One without relatives doesn't cook corn-broth on stones (because nobody holds the cooking pot and he therefore can't stir the broth). Meaning: Whoever has no relatives or friends is a person deserving sympathy.

By stipulating that the children of their enslaved wives should be among those to receive money or property upon their deaths, slave owners were simply following the ethical norms that governed how individuals in their society *should* behave. That this change came after the British abolished slavery and attacked the continued existence of a local trade in domestic slaves was no accident. For while local proverbs expressed sympathy for the enslaved, it was the rhetoric employed by the British government and the actions of the German missionaries who worked in the Anlo area that offered direction on how one should act upon those sympathies.

Colonial officers tasked with the responsibility of explaining to their colonial subjects British policies on the abolition of the slave trade emphasized in their exchanges with local chiefs that a distinction *had* to be made between domestic animals and men, women, and children. One "[could] buy fowls . . . pigs . . . [and] sheep," but African leaders had to "put a stop to the buying and selling of men, women and children."[27] German missionary practices emphasized even more clearly that those of slave descent were to be respected based not on their social origins, but rather on their accomplishments. They regularly praised the work of locals on whom they relied. Without their support, they would have found it impossible to carry out missionary work in Anlo. So many of these individuals were of slave descent. Perhaps most significantly, in 1881 they ordained as pastor, Rudolph Mallet, a former slave, elevating him to the same status as themselves.[28] This could not have gone unnoticed.

Tamakloe embraced these changes. He made no distinctions between his own children and those of his former slaves when he offered all of them the opportunity to obtain schooling free of charge. He selected those among his extended family to whom he provided support so they could further their education in Britain not on the basis of their social origins, but rather on their scholarly accomplishments. Using his status as a prominent and well respected chief, he went even further than this. By 1898, he obtained official recognition from the Gold Coast colonial government for the formerly enslaved leaders of the villages where he settled those whom he had captured in war or had purchased.[29] The Anlo local government officially accepted all three as well, and granted them the title of village head (*hanua*). This gave them the right to establish courts to settle disputes, and the right to have their voices and that of their fellow formerly enslaved community members heard in matters that concerned the entire polity.

Why did Tamakloe take this approach? Did the rhetoric of the British and the actions of the German missionaries resonate with him? Or did it simply make sense for Tamakloe to do this as part of a larger strategy to pursue his economic and political goals? As indicated Tamakloe invested in a number of different enterprises, both in Anlo and in the wider region. The need for labor to pursue these activities, however, was an ever present reality. Bodies were needed to produce the copra and palm oil that was in demand in Europe. They were also need to process, transport and sell these commodities. Those entrepreneurs involved in both production and trade, like Tamakloe, also needed educated individuals to serve as accountants and bookkeepers. What better way to produce loyal workers than to provide ones former slaves—those who had already been incorporated into one's extended family—with unprecedented educational opportunities And at a time when Tamakloe was among those who were pushing the political leadership in Anlo to embrace what they believed were the benefits of the British colonial presence, what better way to further this agenda than by elevating ones loyal former slave community heads to positions within the Anlo traditional council so they too could add their voices to the advice given to the then notoriously conservative Anlo political leader, Awoamefia Amedor Kpegla. Tamakloe may have been influenced by the ideas and practices of the British and the German missionaries in the area, but he also knew how to take advantage of the abolition of slavery in ways that allowed him to promote his economic and political interests.

But are these factors all that explain why Tamakloe broke with the social norms in terms of how he handled the colonial abolition of slavery? Was there something more personal that undergirded his approach to the formerly enslaved? Paul Sands, one of Tamakoe's closest advisors, the person who "[wrote] all his documents and necessary papers" was of slave descent himself. Tamakloe would have certainly known of Sands's origins. Other people certainly did, even the children in the community who publicly taunted him. Would Tamakloe have known about the bitterness Sands felt at being abused because of his social origins? Did Sands express these feelings not only in his diary, but also to Tamakloe? Their frequent contact, the trust that necessarily had to exist between them, would have provided Sands with the opportunity to share with Tamakloe these most intimate questions and concerns. But did he? And did this, in turn, allow him to reassess how he thought about the institution of slavery and those of slave descent?

Whatever the answers to these questions may be, Tamakloe acted in accordance with—but also at times in advance of—the changing views of other slaveholders. He did so, however, on the basis of his own priorities and concerns. Tamakloe, like other former slave masters in Anlo, never formally freed his slaves. That he left to British colonial policy. Still, his approach differed from others in the way he handled those who he had once enslaved. As mentioned, the majority of slave owners in Anlo adjusted by altering the way they interacted with their former slaves. They absorbed them as junior branches of their own lineages; and when referring to the formerly enslaved in conversation, slave masters used euphemisms that would not be insulting if their words got back to the persons about whom they were speaking.[30] Still, by using such euphemisms, they could quietly identify to the listener the social identity of formerly enslaved individuals. This was especially necessary in Anlo because so many knew where they came from, having been recently captured in the 1869 war in Krepi. If insulted, they could simply leave. And in leaving, they would deprive their masters of the labor force that was so necessary to engage in business at a time when free labor was quite scarce. Discretion was the order of the day. Tamakloe, however, appears to have handled this question of how best to manage the formerly enslaved by pursuing a very different path. As noted, he didn't formally free his slaves, but he gave them every incentive to want to remain with him and in the area. He provided free educational opportunities for them through the Catholic Church; he elevated the formerly enslaved to positions of leadership that gave them an opportunity to have a say not only in their own villages, but within the larger counsel of chiefs. He gave them an opportunity to obtain a degree of respect in

Anlo that might not have been available to them even if they did return to their former homes.

Tamakloe as Politician

Tamakloe, like many other chiefs in Anlo, was initially hostile to the British government. He fought against them at Atiteti and Agoue and in the Glover war. He also eschewed converting to Christianity, the religion of the British colonizers. Instead, as the sponsor of three different Yewe religious orders and as a practitioner of the Afa divination system,[31] he maintained his allegiance to Anlo traditional religious practices and beliefs until the last years of his life. But after he and the Anlo leadership came to the conclusion that they were unable to militarily resist the coming of British colonial rule, Tamakloe, as noted, focused intensely on his business interests, documenting with care many of his transactions while also giving tremendous support for the expansion of Western education in Anlo as provided by several different Christian missionary societies. One would assume, given this level of engagement with both the colonial system and missionary endeavors, that archival records would be replete with information about him. That is not the case, however. There is relatively little mention of Tamakloe in the Bremen and British colonial records I have consulted to date. Despite his quite prominent status in the area as both a respected military leader and a wealthy businessman, he seems to have avoided much daily involvement with either the Bremen-based Norddeutschen Missionsgesellschaft (NDMG) or the British government. What we do know from these few sources and from oral histories is that Tamakloe was relentlessly pragmatic.

In oral histories, he is remembered for his saying *"Yevu kutsa de wodia nutsi"* (The Europeans are like the sponge; they make your skin smooth). In other words, Europeans and their ideas had their uses, ones that could be beneficial to himself and to Anlo.[32] That this was precisely the approach he took was noted by the British colonial governor H. T. Ussher when he met Tamakloe in 1879 in Keta. As Ussher noted: "I had an interview this morning with Chief Tamaklo, an influential and powerful chief of Awunah. He appeared to me only to be here and friendly on account of the personal interest he has in property both here and at Denoe."[33] In this interview, Ussher had sought to persuade Tamakloe to help him organize a personal meeting with the Anlo paramount chief to encourage him to help stop the smuggling of alcohol, guns, and gunpowder that, according to Ussher, was ruining the profits of legitimate traders in the Addah area. But as noted by Ussher, Tamakloe "was extremely averse, and the whole of his body language proved conclusively that he was only trimming. He objected [to arranging such a meeting] on various grounds . . . that sundry things were against the king's fetish, that this and that was not customary for them." Tamakloe's objections may indeed have been legitimate, but his own business interests would also have strongly encouraged him to take this stance. While Tamakloe was ostensibly "friendly" to the British colonial government, he was actually more interested in using it to enhance his own financial concerns than anything else. By 1899, for example, he encouraged the British to officially recognize the chief of Klikor, a neighboring district that was part of Greater Anlo.[34] This allowed the chief to receive a stipend from the British government. This stipend, however, unlike that given to the chiefs in Central Anlo,[35] was in the form of liquor rather than money. On pushing for the official recognition of the Klikor chief, Tamakloe then arranged to "buy [from the Klikor chief] the [sum of the] liquor that the British government was granting government-affiliated chiefs in lieu of financial payments . . . at a very low cost." Tamakloe would then sell this liquor or supply it to other retailers and then provide those retailers with the information they needed to avoid being caught if they wished to smuggle the liquor out of the territory without paying tariffs.[36] Tamakloe would have reaped great profits from this scheme, even though he was ostensibly serving as a government-recognized chief, upholding British colonial law.

Tamakloe used the British government for his own interests in an equally surreptitious way when he supported the opening of trade between the coast and the interior. The long-standing trade ties that had formerly linked the region known as Krepi with the coast had been abruptly suspended in 1869 after Anlo aligned itself with Asante to wreak devastation on the Krepi area. Merchants on the Anlo coast, including Tamakloe, were keenly interested in reestablishing business ties with these communities, which were thought to be potentially rich in the vegetable oils, cotton, and rubber that were in so much demand on the international market. Loss of access to this region had meant that the Anlos' competitors in Accra to the west, and Anecho to the east, were the only ones able to benefit financially from trade with that area.

The Anlo merchants based in Keta were not the only ones interested in reestablishing trade ties, however. So, too, was the British government. It wanted to reopen trade between Krepi and Keta so as to direct the commodities produced in the interior to Keta rather than to the coastal towns further east where German and French commercial interests were dominant.[37] It was under these circumstances that Tamakloe, who had no interest in the British except insofar as he "could use them like a sponge," supported a British sponsored expedition in 1885 to the interior towns to negotiate peace, reconciliation, and renewed trade ties. Already in 1884, Tamakloe had established a store in Asadame on the north side of the lagoon. This would allow him easy access to the goods that would be coming from the interior if trade negotiations were successful.

Yet Tamakloe never publicly associated himself with this British-organized effort. Instead, he stood in the background and offered silent support to those who were prepared to work publicly with the British. It was Joachim Acolatse, Tamakloe's uncle and friend, for example, who took the lead in openly advocating for the resumption of trade on this route. Paul Sands, with whom Tamakloe was very closely associated, did the same and actually participated in the expedition. But Tamakloe demurred. For while he sought to take advantage of every new opportunity that came his way, he had no interest in alienating those with whom he was associated in other ways. The Anlo chiefs resident in the towns on the north side of the Keta Lagoon (which separated the Anlo littoral from Anlo's interior towns and villages) saw the British trade expedition into the interior as a major threat to their own political and economic interests. Keta, located on the Atlantic littoral, was not only the major center of commerce in Anlo, but also the seat of the British colonial government in the region. In reviving the interior-coastal trade under British auspices, the chiefs from the interior Anlo towns feared the expansion of British rule and their even more intrusive interference in the smuggling of goods that had become an essential part of the north-side lagoon towns' income-producing activities. Tamakloe understood the concerns of these chiefs and thus took no public stance on the issue, but from his perspective, it was possible to live with British colonial rule while taking advantage of it. Despite efforts by the interior Anlo towns to prevent the expedition, it took place and was successful in reopening trade ties. But the cost of this success was a deep split between the merchants and chiefs resident in the towns on Anlo's littoral and those situated north of the Keta Lagoon. Efforts by Tamakloe to heal this breech failed, but the words he uttered in frustration about the attitudes of the chiefs from the north-side towns and their obdurate opposition to the British reveal yet again how he saw in the British, opportunities that if seized could be of great benefit to himself and to the Anlo polity. For Tamakloe, opposition to British colonial rule had proven to be impossible. The only question that remained was how best to gain from their presence while minimizing its damaging effects. That meant supporting Western education so that one could better negotiate with and thereby protect one's interests in this new era. It meant taking advantage of the much greater economic opportunities offered by the expansion of trade that was fostered by the British colonial presence. And it meant for him, as he stated quite explicitly, that those who could not or would not understand this approach were simply "ignorant"; they were people who so disliked the white man that they "would not hear [his] words."[38]

When the then Anlo *awoamefia*, Amedor Kpegla died in 1906, Tamakloe saw this as yet another opportunity to relentlessly pursue the course he had forged for himself and the Anlo polity. The responsibility for filling the office of *awoamefia* rotated between two clans, the Bate and the Adzovia. Because Amedor Kpegla was from the Bate clan, it was now the turn of the Adzovia, Tamakloe's clan, to elect the leader who would influence the future of the polity for as long as that person reigned. Tamakloe was in a particularly strong position to influence the choice. His credentials were impeccable. On his father's side, he traced his descent to respected leaders in his hometown of Whuti; on his mother's side he was a descendant of Wenya, the leader of the Ewe-speaking immigrants who founded the Anlo polity.[39] He was also a deeply respected military leader who had been accorded, because of his valor, the many praise names (known as drinking names, *ahanonkowo*) that opened this chapter. He was also frequently referred to in local songs as "rich Tamakloe," because he had accumulated so much money he was able to sponsor the establishment of many different traditional religious shrine houses in the area.[40] Given the opportunity to influence who would be the next *awoamefia*, Tamakloe was certainly not going to allow this "animal [i.e., this opportunity] that visited his farm to return with [even] its feet." Thus, it was Tamakloe who is remembered as having chosen the next *awoamefia* on behalf of the Adzovia clan and then sending his own son with the delegation to inform the candidate of the decision.[41]

The person selected, Cornelius Kofi Kwawukume, had been educated at the Bremen mission school in Keta, and had been working first as an assistant with the mission and then as a self-employed trader/businessman in German Cameroon. The choice was certainly influenced by the fact that, as one local resident remembered in the 1930s, "prior to the [1907] installation of Fia Sri II, [in the 1880s and '90s] the nation was itching for educated and civilized chieftaincy."[42] Many chiefs, especially Tamakloe, felt it was extremely important to have the polity's interests represented by someone who was familiar with the colonial system. They also felt, like Tamakloe, that if Anlo was to prosper, it had to modernize.[43] On his appointment to the office, Sri II immediately began to do just that. He broke with the traditions that had governed the office by shortening the period for the installation rituals. He refused to abide by the tradition that forced the *awoamefia* to seclude himself from public view. He wore Western-style sewn clothing and lifted the ban on such attire for Anlo citizens in Anloga, the Anlo capital, which had been enforced as late as the rule of his predecessor, Amedor Kpegla.[44] In subsequent years, he worked closely with the British colonial government to modernize the local governance system, and the layout and sanitary conditions of Anlo towns and villages.[45] Tamakloe was one of the closest advisors and supporters of Fia Sri II. And Fia Sri also supported Tamakloe. This is perhaps most evident with regard to Tamakloe's actions against the cultural system that stigmatized those of slave descent. When Fia Sri II came into office, he maintained recognition of the former slaves whom Tamakloe had persuaded the traditional council in the 1890s to officially accept as the heads of their villages. When a decision in Tamakloe's court was appealed for final judgment to

Fia Sri II in 1914, he again upheld Tamakloe's decision that the former owner of a slave couple had no right, as a master would have had in the past, to dictate to that couple's children who they should marry.[46]

Again, we must ask, what prompted Tamakloe to take such a prominent and public stance against the stigma of slave origins? The British colonial government had made it quite clear that it opposed the institution of slavery and regularly gave refuge to the enslaved in Anlo who sought to free themselves from their masters. Did rhetoric about the repugnancy of slavery speak to Tamakloe even though he had participated in both the capture of men, women, and children and their enslavement, as well as in the purchase of enslaved individuals from markets in the region? Or was it the threat of potentially losing his labor force if they returned home? Did the service and loyalty of the many slaves who were sent by their more wealthy Anlo masters to serve in the many campaigns in which he participated later lead him to be more sympathetic to the views of the enslaved, who certainly felt the stigma of their social origins? Did his very close association with and reliance on members of the Euro-African community—many of whom, like Paul Sands, were of slave descent—encourage him to respect such individuals because he needed their talents to ensure his business success no matter their social status? And did this, in turn, allow him to reassess how he thought about the institution of slavery and those of slave descent? Or was he genuinely touched by their concern about the lack of respect they received in their communities? How much were his views and actions governed by political and business concerns, how much by the personal?

Tamakloe as Sentimentalist

Tamakloe had many wives. One of them was from Ho. She would have been among a number of women who had been enslaved during the 1869–71 war in Krepi. None of these women, including Tamakloe's wife, returned home even though their communities were not that distant. They remained even after 1884 when Anlo resumed trade relations with Krepi. As wives, these women were in a particularly intimate position to convey the pain and anguish of their loss, having been removed and prevented from returning to their natal families even if they now opted to remain in their masters' homes. They were also well placed to win the affections of their husbands. During the nineteenth century, free wives in Anlo were known to have taken full advantage of the opportunity presented by husbands who had enslaved wives to reinforce their ties to their own natal families. These women spent much time in their fathers' and brothers' households, visiting, assisting their relatives with their businesses, encouraging their children to know and work for their uncles so the children could benefit from the ties they had to both their maternal and paternal relations. Enslaved wives had no such opportunities. They had been forcibly separated from their own families and incorporated against their will into the households of their masters/husbands. In light of this situation, many enslaved women opted willingly to work harder for their husbands than others in the household, to please them as best they could, in order to secure their own positions and that of their children in the hearts of those who had sole control over their fates. That such strategies worked is frequently mentioned by Anlo elders familiar with the history of slavery and that of their own families.

> [The slaves] were regarded . . . as [the masters'] own children. In fact, they regarded them more. . . . They gave them even more in inheritance of property. Because [the children of a slave wife] had no uncle or aunt, they had no other source. If [the master] became involved in a war, your own children [had] aunts and uncles to help them [avoid going to war], but the slave [had] no one. If a sacrifice [was] to be made, the aunts and uncles [would] tell their nieces and nephews [to be careful], but the slave [had] no one to tell him to run away. That's why [slave masters gave] them more.[47]
>
> My actual grandfather . . . had slaves. He bought 3 women and distributed them to his cousins and a brother to marry. He brought them when he returned from the battlefield at Kpetoe [during the 1869–71 war in Krepi]. The children of these women were very serviceable to . . . my father so he gave all from his paternal side to them and my family got only the maternal side for inheritance. Anything he asked, they would do it.[48]

While these two reminiscences emphasize the extent to which enslaved women were able to so endear themselves and their children to their masters that they received—over and above the children of their free co-wives—the bulk of their master's inheritance, that does not seem to have been the approach taken by Tamakloe. He did not make a distinction between the children of his enslaved and free wives, or between these boys and girls and the children of the slave parents whom he had owned. He made no such distinction when making educational opportunities available to them. He continued this approach when selecting those in whom he placed his greatest trust.[49] Still, it is clear that Tamakloe felt special affection toward certain individuals. He seems to have been close to the brother and nephew who were lost in the Agoue and Glover wars, respectively; he was described by a local Anlo author as close to his beloved cousin, Old Amega, who died in 1898.[50] According to Bremen missionary E. J. Reinke, he was especially close to one of his wives. In his 1904 report, he noted: "Chief Tamakloe['s] wife, a good Christian woman, had died many years ago and her death made him [especially] sorrowful. In a letter to his son-in-law, he further expressed his melancholy, and also how excited he would be if he could see his wife again in the afterlife."[51] Such expressions of sentimentality were not unusual in Anlo. They were frequently shared in private with family and friends, but also found public expression in the songs (dirges and laments) that were very popular in the area.[52] That Tamakloe was particularly close to one of his wives would also not have been unusual. But who was she? And in what ways might she have so endeared herself to him that he still mourned losing her years after her death? Could she have been one of his wives who had been enslaved and who was thus in a position to convey to him what it meant to lose not only relatives through war (as he had) but also to lose one's relatives through enslavement? We may never know.

More important is that Tamakloe knew what it meant to lose someone with whom he was very close even before the death of this particular wife. This alone could have made him sensitive to the plight of the enslaved. But other experiences and elements in his life also probably contributed to his efforts to undermine the social stigma of slavery. Exposure to the antislave trade and slavery rhetoric of the British and the German missionaries working in the area; experiencing the loss of life not only of his close relatives, and beloved wife, but also the death of the loyal and brave troops under his command, many of whom were of slave descent; and knowing of the taunts suffered by one of his closest advisors who, too, was of slave descent—certainly must have played a role in altering his view about slavery.

Perhaps most important of all, Tamakloe was willing and able to reassess and alter his views on a variety of matters. He then used his considerable prestige to push for change within the larger community. Others exposed to the very same influences, others with a similar status and background did not take this path. Only Tamakloe. As indicated, he had no love for the British. He fought against them in the Atiteti war; he fought against them in the Agoue war. And he lost relatives and men to British fire in both. Yet he was willing to reconsider how he viewed this once fierce enemy. Instead of maintaining implacable opposition, he shifted to a more utilitarian position by focusing on taking advantage of their presence. He utilized their legal system to secure his property rights while at the same time ignoring those laws when they did not suit his economic interests. He accepted land, but also people (despite the British ban on both the institutions of slavery and debt peonage) as collateral when giving loans to individuals in need of cash. When a lender was unable to pay, he incorporated both pawns and lands into his holdings.[53] When the colonial government established a system of indirect rule in which local chiefs were authorized to manage the affairs of their communities under fairly loose government supervision, Tamakloe managed to have his position as chief recognized in both his hometown of Whuti as well as in Keta. When the British began paying these chiefs stipends, Tamakloe was able to secure for himself the highest amount, only second to the stipend given to the Anlo paramount chief, the *awoamefia*. And when these colonial stipends were extended in the form of liquor instead of cash to the chiefs in communities outside the immediate Anlo polity, he was able to take advantage of this system to encourage the British government to recognize those chiefs from whom he could purchase this liquor at a much lower rate than would have been possible on the open market. He then resold it for a significant profit either outside the British controlled area or within the British Gold Coast colony by either smuggling it in or selling it to smugglers without paying the hefty duties that were imposed on imported liquor. He did all this while remaining in the good graces of the British government. When the British expressed an interest in reestablishing trade ties with the Krepi towns in the interior, he supported the effort, surreptitiously again, because it served his interests to do so in this way. He openly embraced Western education, however. In doing all this, Tamakloe broke with whatever past hostilities he may have had toward Europeans and embraced instead the notion that they were like a sponge; they could be used to benefit one's own interests and make the Anlo polity better.

So, too, it seems Tamakloe broke with the prevailing attitudes about those of slave status. Knowing how important those individuals were to the production of his own wealth and that of others, but tempered by his understanding of the anguish of losing of one's natal relatives, and aware of the pain experienced by some of those closest to him who were taunted for something over which they had no control, he modified his views on slavery. In his own family, he refused to distinguish between slave and free; in his courts he upheld the notion that those of slave descent could successfully sue those who abused them because of their origins; and as a member of the traditional council of chiefs, he supported the official recognition of a number of his former slaves as heads of their own communities. Convinced that this was the right path, he broke with a centuries-old tradition that accepted slavery as part of the fabric of life. He then forged a new path that he believed would "make [Anlo] beautiful."

Legacies

This was Tamakloe's approach. It would appear, however, that after his death in 1918, not everyone in his family was prepared to follow his lead. Providing educational and low-level leadership opportunities to the formerly enslaved was one thing. It was quite another, however, to allow a former slave to inherit the prestigious chieftaincy position that Tamakloe had held during his lifetime. To do so would have gone against still strongly held local norms. It would have created a level playing field when it was certainly in the interest of some to maintain a distinction between slave and free. Evidence of past family rifts are difficult to obtain. Most kin groups avoid making public the internal wranglings that can occur when differences over inheritance arise. Disputes can too easily be used by others who seek their own advantage at the expense of the entire family. Differences can become so bitter, however, that they do become public. This is what occurred in Ghana in 1995 and in Senegal in 2007 when disagreements between former slave and free branches of two different extended families burst onto the public stage as one faction used the courts and the news media to discredit the claims of the other. No such public airing appears to have taken place among Tamakloe's descendants. Rather, the differences that did emerge manifested themselves in the inordinate length of time it took for the family to install a successor to the *miafiaga* stool that Nyaho Tamakloe had held. After his death in 1918, it took twenty-five years for the family to agree to abide by his will with regard to his successor. Long periods in which a stool remains vacant is not unusual in Ghana's history. What *is* remarkable is that after these twenty-five years, his descendants did, indeed, make no distinctions among Tamakoe's descendants based on social origins. His successor, Julius Michael Tamakloe, enstooled as Tamakloe II, was the son of a woman from Tokokoe, near Ho, whom Tamakloe married after capturing her in the 1869–71 war.[54] That A. W. Kuetuade-Tamaklo, descendant of Nyaho Tamakloe, shared this information publically and freely, is indicative as well that for this family the paternal connection as well as a candidate's knowledge and skills were far more important than enslaved origins on the maternal side in determining who should inherit Nyaho Tamakloe's position as *miafiaga* of Anlo and as Tamakloe family head.[55]

Did the approach taken by Tamakloe and his descendants encourage other families to follow their lead? It is difficult to say without more extensive research. What we do know is that they were not alone in their willingness to de-emphasize the importance of slave origins. In her study of a group of communities in the Senegal River Valley, historian Jean Schmitz identified an extended family that, like Tamakloe, provided a number of their former slaves with unprecedented opportunities to improve their status, while also maintaining the extended family through a range of patronage gestures. After abolition, Schmitz indicates that two members of the Wan family, Ibraa Almaami and Aamadu Moktar, gave to a number of their former slaves land on which they could work, not as sharecroppers, however, as was more common, but land that they could claim as their own. This same family also established with one of their former slaves "a milk kinship," a social relationship that "obfuscated the memory of the slave master relation" and one that was characterized by "greater egalitarianism and affection." As noted by Schmitz, these acts—like the educational opportunities offered by Tamakloe—provided the formerly enslaved with "concrete avenues of social mobility."[56] In southwestern Ghana, the situation was somewhat different, but here too, those of free status refused to allow the stigma of slave origins to block the social and political mobility of those of slave descent when such openness served their purposes.[57] Historian Pierluigi Valsecchi notes that, "such individuals [could] climb up the power structures in both the economic and politico-institutional spheres." In other words, slave status was never a bar for holding high political office among the Nzema. In fact, in many instances, such individuals were so preferred that "an amazing number of Nzema successors to high office had non-free ancestry" during the precolonial and colonial periods, until the 1930s when a group of presumably free royals successfully passed a law that prohibited sexual unions between royals and slave women. It was in the 1940s that this law was challenged, and by the time of Ghana's independence, in 1957, the law was scrapped and the older system reinstated. Significantly, the stigma associated with slave origins has remained among the Nzema, but no one publicly discusses the origins of such individuals. Instead, silence has allowed the various chieftaincies to "return to a tradition" in which Nzema royal families refuse to allow slave origins to bar family members of slave descent from holding traditional political offices.[58]

Opposition to the debilitating stigmatization of those of slave descent certainly has not rested solely on the shoulders of former slave-owning families like the Tamakloes of Ghana and the Wans of Senegal, or the royal families of Nzema. In fact, it has been the formerly enslaved themselves who have been the most active in battling the negative images that have clung to them because of their origins. Throughout the late nineteenth and twentieth century, they immigrated to other areas to begin life anew; took advantage of both colonial and Islamic educational opportunities to improve their status; renegotiated their relations with their former masters; and invested heavily in their own labor in an effort (sometimes successful) to lift themselves out of poverty.[59] And it was they who most actively used in other places in West Africa the anticolonial rhetoric—first in the 1950s and '60s, and again in the 1990s and early 2000s in the wake of the push for democratization—to challenge their continued stigmatization and to demand real freedom from slavery and full citizenship rights.[60] Still, the willingness of a few like Tamakloe and his descendants to support the formerly enslaved and those of slave descent was and continues to be important. Their efforts increased the opportunities for that first generation of formerly enslaved individuals who were able to seize these openings to invest in their own futures. Because of those opportunities, many were also able to establish a foundation upon which their own descendants would continue to build.

3 Noah Yawo of Ho-Kpenoe

The Faith Journey of a Slave Owner

> Anybody who has 8 to 10 sheep is referred to as a rich man. Even if he has only
> five sheep, a person is rich, especially if he also has some goats, chicken and
> pigs. When he lends 40 marks to somebody, this person becomes his pledge; if
> he lends another about 100 marks, this person also becomes his pledge as well.
> Such a man is rich. . . . This type of rich person buys slaves and marries many
> wives. When a festival is celebrated, and he wants to show off, he distributes
> beautiful clothes among his children, cooks a good meal and makes available a
> lot of palm wine for people to drink. . . . He buys guns and gun powder for his
> children and pawns. His bowls are full of cowry-shells. He lives in a spacious
> house, and has plantations of yams, maize and cassava. Anyone who can do all
> this is a rich man.
>
> —Jakob Spieth, *The Ewe People*[1]

THERE IS NO better description for the man known as Yawo, who came from
the village of Ho-Kpenoe in what is now southeastern Ghana. As a well-known
businessman and farmer, he was indeed wealthy. He did not have the kinds of
assets possessed by Amegashie Afeku or Tamakloe. Still, in 1862, he was known
in his community as a well-to-do slave owner.[2] Yawo had the financial resources
not only to buy men, women, and children at the busy markets in the area, but
to marry and maintain three wives. His household included all these individuals, as well as a number of debt pawns, individuals given to him temporarily, to
serve as both collateral and as workers, by those to whom he had lent money. He
conducted business in his home area, and as far afield as the towns of Agotime
and Kpando, about twenty-six and sixty kilometers respectively, from his village of Kpenoe.[3] Yet, in 1875, some thirteen years later, Yawo abandoned it all.
He divorced two of his wives. He renounced slave ownership and stated publicly
that he would acquire no new slaves. In addition, he agreed to free the children
of his slaves, and to allow the adults to redeem themselves. In other words, "he
gave away . . . much money."[4] How did someone like Yawo come to make such
a momentous decision? What prompted him to abandon everything that he
had worked for, to eschew the markers of success that had been defined by his

Noah Yawo. Courtesy of the Norddeutsche Mission.

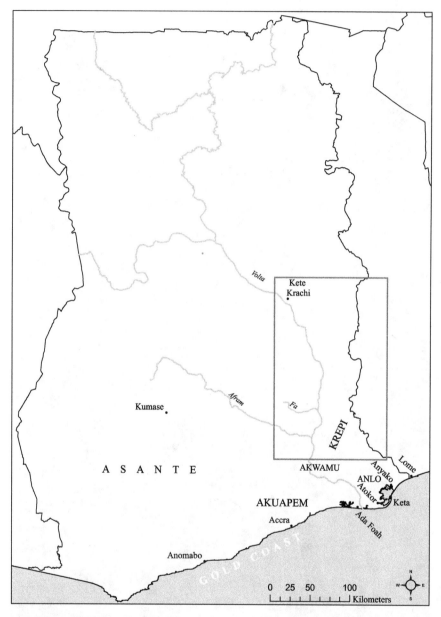

Krepi and other polities in West Africa/Ghana

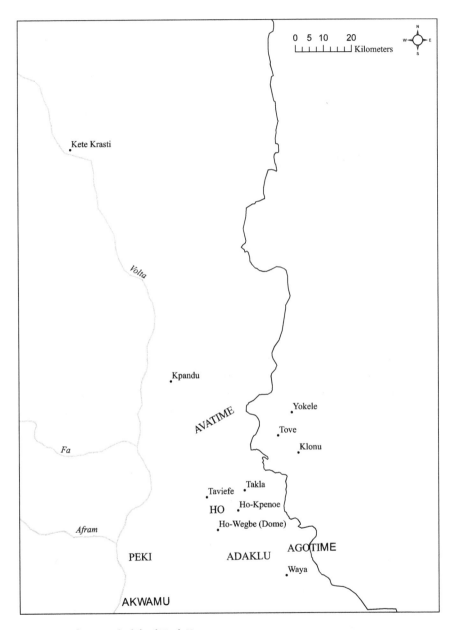

Towns significant in the life of Noah Yawo

community? Certainly, his conversion to Christianity was a factor. But not all converts were prepared to divorce all their wives but one, let alone emancipate their slaves.[5] Yawo, himself, did so reluctantly, but he did it nevertheless. Why? A number of events seem to have influenced his decision, many of which deeply affected him: an earthquake, war, disease, famine, death. By documenting the history of the Ho region in the nineteenth century, and how Yawo interpreted the events that so impacted him and others, this chapter explores how a cascade of events could generate in Yawo a crisis of faith, and propel him to completely alter how he positioned himself in the world.

Years of War, Years of Prosperity: Ho in the 1830s to about 1860

Although we know virtually nothing about Yawo's early years, he was likely born in the 1830s, a time of great upheaval in the region.[6] His hometown, Kpenoe, was part of the polity of Ho, which in turn existed (along with a multiplicity of other small, Ewe-speaking, independent polities) in a region known in the eighteenth and nineteenth centuries as Krepi.[7] The residents in this region had long been beset by a range of threats. Land disputes, failed business deals, and minor quarrels escalated not infrequently into open warfare.[8] The region also suffered from frequent and brutal military aggression by the more powerful states of Akwamu and Asante. Their steady demands for the payment of tribute brought hardships, and when Krepi residents offered passive resistance, they were met with military retaliation and enslavement.[9] Armed revolts against Akwamu and Asante predations were not uncommon.[10] The most successful of these came in the 1820s and '30s, the time of Yawo's birth, when the peoples of Krepi finally freed themselves from both Akwamu and Asante rule.

Krepi independence could not have come at a better time. During this same period, trade opportunities had increased tremendously for those in the region, due largely to developments on the coast. Some thirty years earlier, in 1807, Britain had abolished the slave trade. It then deployed a squadron of ships off the West African coast to prohibit the export of slaves from the region. Sales of enslaved men, women, and children dropped precipitously. Success for British antislavery activists, however, meant serious problems for the inland power of Asante, which had traditionally sent their human exports for sale to the Gold Coast ports of Anamaboe, Cape Coast, and Accra. Unable to find sufficient European buyers for its slaves, and prohibited by the local African communities located on the coast from purchasing the firearms and gunpowder that they believed Asante would use to extend its imperial power over their own independent polities, Asante sought alternative ports.[11] The coastal area east of the Volta proved to be quite attractive. There, the Volta River provided a convenient route on which to convey goods between the interior and the coast. And those to the west of the river who had imposed the embargo on the sale of weaponry to Asante controlled neither the river nor the many land routes that connected this portion of the coast to the interior.[12] The result: trade east of the Volta between the coast and the interior increased tremendously. This upsurge occurred in the 1830s, during the very same time that Krepi gained its independence from Akwamu and Asante.[13] No longer could these two impose tolls on all traders who used the roads in the region, nor could they continue to monopolize the market for slaves and ivory while also demanding tribute in slaves from the conquered. Now free, the small polities in Krepi were able to take advantage of the increase in trade that was conveyed through the region. Benefiting the most was Ho: "traders came more regularly . . . and . . . eventually [it] became the most important trading center in the entire [K]repe area."[14] Yet impediments remained.

Immediately to the south of Krepi was the polity of Anlo, long a trade partner with those to the north.[15] But as the prohibition on the export of slaves on the Gold Coast forced those involved in this trade to shift their operations east of the Volta River, Anlo sought to strengthen its highly profitable middleman position by making it difficult for the traders from the Krepi interior to exchange their goods directly with the Europeans and Euro-Africans operating on their section of the Atlantic coast.[16] The people of Ho responded by expanding their coastal business ties to buyers located to the east and west of Anlo (even though this made their trips longer and therefore more costly), and to the north. They also warmly welcomed to Ho the presence of a new set of strangers, European missionaries.

Since 1847 the German Nordeutschen Missions-Gesellschaft (NDMG) had been working in areas east of the Volta among the many different Ewe-speaking communities. Based largely in the Anlo coastal town of Keta after 1852, the NDMG decided to expand its evangelical efforts to the peoples in the interior. Its missionaries began by establishing a station in Waya in 1855, about eighty-six kilometers northeast of Keta. In 1859 they sought permission to begin work in Ho. The political leader there, Fia Motey Kofi, received them most warmly.[17] He did so, however, not because he was interested in the Christian religion, but because a missionary presence in Ho gave the local residents an opportunity to establish good relations with outsiders whom they perceived could help them overcome Anlo dominance of the trade with the Europeans in Keta. From its early beginnings, the NDMG had been closely associated with the business of trade. Deeply involved in support of the mission's activities was German businessman, J. W. Vietor, a member of its board of directors. In 1857, just two years before the NDMG established its station at Ho, Vietor had dispatched a ship to Brazil to purchase goods for export to Europe. To support the NDMG's mission in West Africa, however, the ship was directed to stop at Keta to bring supplies to the missionaries there. To the ship captain's surprise, he was able to purchase in Keta enough goods to fill the entire hold of his ship, making the onward trip to Brazil unnecessary. When the ship returned to Keta on a second voyage, it brought a missionary employee, C. Rotmann, "whose sole purpose would be commercial." As noted by historian Peter Bühler:

> [Rotmann's] title was of mission procurist, and his purpose [was] to manage [the] supply needs [of the missionaries in West Africa]. It was his province to order the necessary goods from Bremen through the Vietor Company, and to render the process as inexpensive as possible in order not to drain mission funds. The most appropriate way seemed to be through the institution of trade with Ewes through the exchange of European goods for African [palm] oil. The oil was then exported to Europe through the Bremen Factorei, which supplied the mission with its everyday needs. The economic implications of the connection between the NDMG and C. Rotmann . . . are clear. First, the mission became directly involved in commerce through their affiliation. Second, [Rotmann's] presence drew the attention of hinterland Ewes. Those . . . like the [political leader of Ho, who] wished to establish direct connections with European traders, now could do so through the mission.[18]

That a missionary presence could offer to the people of Ho and others in the region an alternative outlet for trade was understood not only by Fia Motey Kofi, but also by the Anlo.

When the Europeans associated with the NDMG first began moving into the interior, the Anlo (more specifically those from the town of Anyako who had been quite successful up to that time in limiting the access of traders from the interior to traders on the Anlo coast) did their best to sabotage the Mission's expansion efforts.[19] In 1856, for example, when the NDMG began their work in Adaklu-Waya by erecting—with the permission of the local political authorities—a house from which to base their efforts, the Anlo encouraged the Adaklu workers, who were helping the missionaries, to strike for higher wages in order to at least delay construction. When this proved ineffective, a fire mysteriously tore through the building rendering it uninhabitable. Much was at stake, economically, for those Anlos whose profits from trade depended on maintaining their middleman position between the interior and the Europeans on the coast. But great opportunity existed for those in the interior if they could break the Anlo trade monopoly. Thus, when the NDMG missionaries first entered Ho, they found Fia Motey Kofi "well disposed" toward them and quite willing to sell them land on which to build their mission.

Among those in Ho who took advantage of the new opportunities for trade that had emerged after the 1830s when Ho freed itself of Akwamu and Asante control was Yawo of Ho-Kpenoe. Although primarily a farmer, he was able to generate enough profits from trading between Ho and towns to the north and south that he could lend money to others, while also establishing and maintaining a household of three wives, two debt pawns, and at least one slave.[20] This was no small feat. Trading during this period could be dangerous. Indebtedness was quite common and this could have serious consequences not only for the indebted person, but for everyone associated with that individual. Lenders like Yawo who were unable to recover their loans often resorted to kidnapping (also called panyarring) the relatives or townspeople of the debtor. The lender would then sell those kidnapped into slavery to recover his or her money. If a lender was unable to recover the loan in this way, he or she simply had to absorb the loss no matter how great, but if the lender engaged in kidnapping, it could create such hostility between the lender, and the family and community of the debtor that relations could become severely strained to the point of armed conflict. This system of loan recovery could make travel to other communities by both lender and debtor quite dangerous even in the most peaceful of times. Yawo, however, was undeterred. His willingness to venture beyond the confines of his community, his interest in seizing new business opportunities no matter the risk, and his tendency to embrace fully, and with a certain degree of single-mindedness, the tasks he set for himself made him the wealthy man he became by about 1860.

A Time of Questioning, 1862–68

While the late 1830s, '40s, and '50s were a time of relative peace in the Ho area, with only minor conflicts erupting in the region to disrupt what was otherwise a period of expanding economic opportunity,[21] the 1860s and early 1870s saw Yawo and the people of Ho facing increasingly serious challenges. The first came in 1862. On the 10th of July that year, a powerful earthquake shook the entire region.

As described by Christian Hornberger, a German missionary who was working in the area, the earthquake had a profound impact on Ho's residents: "On the 10th of July, we had an earthquake. . . . Whatever this new phenomenon was, no one knew. . . . Everything was in an uproar in the village. . . . Yawo and his countrymen, . . . who knew so little about an earthquake that their language did not even have a word for it, . . . asked how can this solid earth be so shaken to bits?"[22] Unnerved by what they had experienced, the elders in Ho's different towns immediately demanded a halt to all "work on the enraged mother earth with the hoe."[23] They then sought an explanation for the quake not only from the local priests who lived in their individual towns, but also the European missionaries. This was most unusual. For while the people of Ho had welcomed the Christian workers, their warm embrace was not accompanied by the very thing the missionaries hoped for: conversions to Christianity. The people of Ho were polite to the strangers. They listened to their sermons. They invited them into their homes. A few even attended the morning prayer sessions the missionaries held. None expressed interest in abandoning their own faith for Christianity; and none were prepared to send a child to the school that the missionaries had established. At least not initially.[24] The earthquake that shook the entire region in 1862 marked the beginning of the end of that approach.

On the morning of July 11, 1862, less than twenty-four hours after the quake, Ho's political leader, Fia Motey Kofi, called a meeting of the entire polity. The leaders from each of the five towns that composed the Ho polity,[25] the priests and priestesses, the youth, as well as the missionaries, attended. His purpose: to allow all to hear whatever explanations the local priests and the missionaries could offer as to why the earth had so shaken them. What was the cause of this unprecedented event? The answers offered by both groups were telling. According to NDMG missionary Christian Hornberger who attended the meeting, the local priests consulted one another and then offered the following explanation: "We call the earth our Mother and that she is. But because the white men have been living amongst us already for so long, and they have not given [our gods] even six yards of dark blue cloth, the gods have made the earth shake so because they are angry." Fia Kofi said nothing. He only turned to the missionaries to hear what they had to say. In his response, Hornberger also used the meeting for his own purposes. He harangued the people of Ho for not listening to him and the other missionaries who regularly preached not only in Wegbe (also called Dome), where their station was located, but in the other villages and towns of the Ho polity as well. He then proclaimed the greater power of his God to protect them from whatever might befall them while also warning them of the dire consequences if they failed to listen to him. He remembers saying something like this:

> I thought you wanted to hear the truth, but you called the witnesses [i.e., the local priests] first. Even if I had told you why the earthquake happened, you would still put more faith in the witnesses than in my words, which don't come from me but from the Holy written word. You don't come to our sermons and you don't participate in our devotions. That is why you haven't heard about earthquakes. For us, it is nothing strange, for we read so often about it in God's words. . . . [Hear the word of God:] God made the heavens and the earth and our Father is in heaven. He sends the earthquakes when he sees that the people do not want to hear God's word and prefer instead to sleep in a slumber of old sins. So God often shakes them violently so that they will wake up and begin a new life. We have been preaching to you already two and half years, and you do not want to turn away from the mute tin gods to serve the living God. Therefore, he has shaken you . . . so that you wake up before ruin forces you to do so. . . . And for those who do not take notice of His shaking, there is ever worse to come: stronger earthquakes, terrible hard times, signs in heaven and on earth as in Matthew 24 and the Book of Revelation. . . . I cannot put a stop [to this], any more than the fetish priests and priestesses can stop the earth from shaking them. It will come as it is written, for God's word is Truth and everything else is a lie. Therefore all who do not want to convert should be filled with fear, indeed, filled with great fear. . . . They won't have any helper or savior. But whoever chooses to begin anew and to come to Christ and believe

in Him, has nothing to fear, for the Lord knows His own and He will save them and remain with them. He knows His chosen people and will happily bring them out of every storm.[26]

This harangue does not seem to have impressed many people. But it did not fall on deaf ears either.

The ruling elders in Kpenoe listened intently. They heard Hornberger's words. They heard his predictions. And in response, they decided to begin observing the Christians' day of rest. Everyone in the village was forbidden to work on their farms on Sunday. They were also to refrain from any other economic activity. They were to remain at home.[27] In addition, Kpenoe, and shortly thereafter, Wegbe each decided, for the first time, to send a boy to the missionary school. Concern about earthquakes and a desire to learn more about this unprecedented event may have been a motivating factor, but it certainly was not their only interest. In addition to a new religion and its different ideas about spiritual phenomena, the missionaries also brought alternative building techniques and farming practices that proved to be interesting to the local community. The school curriculum included carpentry, a form of woodworking that, unlike local practices, involved the precise sawing of planks and boards of different sizes, but all uniformly straight, that could then be used to construct European-style doors and windows, beds and chairs, wardrobes and flooring. The European female missionaries who were stationed in Wegbe introduced the art of knitting and European-style sewing.[28] These new ideas, as well as the economic opportunities that the missionary presence promised, came together after the earthquake to generate much more interest in what the missionaries had to say about everything. Among the interested was Yawo's older brother, Gamo. He not only supported the new day of rest and sending a Kpenoe boy to the missionary school in Wegbe, but he also welcomed the missionaries to his home to engage in further discussions about this new faith. Yawo, on the other hand, like the vast majority, remained unmoved.

The July 1862 earthquake was only the first in a series of deeply disturbing challenges the people of Ho were to face. In that same year, 1862, they also had to deal with an especially poor harvest. Yams, the staple crop for the population, were particularly challenging to cultivate. If rainfall was poor, yields were affected negatively. This was especially the case if the type of soil in which the yams were planted was particularly sensitive to rainfall levels.[29] In the Ho town of Heve, agricultural conditions were so difficult by the end of 1862 that many residents feared famine. Coming so soon after the earthquake, this development had the potential of only further damaging the reputations of the local priests, for it was they who had the responsibility for requesting the support of the local gods for a bountiful harvest. Yam cultivation began in the Ho area generally in January or February with the burning of the vegetation that had grown in the fields after the last harvest. The purpose was to supplement the often exhausted soils with additional nutrients from the ash. But the burning also allowed the community to catch the wild animals flushed out of the vegetation by the flames. Prior to such activity, however, it was the priests who were consulted about the sacrifices the hunters must offer to the gods to obtain their help in making the hunt successful. It was the local priests who, after the bush burning, had to "inaugurate the time of planting" with prayers to the gods for the well-being of the people throughout the growing season so that they may "gather in good health" to enjoy a success-ful harvest. And it was the priests who also presided over the yam festival that followed the harvest, but preceded the first consumption of the yams. The failure of the rains to come in sufficient quantity, a poor harvest, or the poor health of the community could be attributed to a number of different reasons: unresolved conflicts within the town; poor sanitation; insufficient or incorrectly offered sac-rifices.[30] None of these reasons would have necessarily encourage community members to lose faith in the power of their gods, but in combination with other difficulties, it could certainly generate questioning, if not doubt.

In light of the drought and concerns about possible famine in Heve, some sought employment with the missionaries. They hoped to use the money earned to purchase food for themselves and their families until they could plant and harvest their own yams during the next season. Others opted to leave the town altogether. They relocated to Wegbe so they could be closer to the mission station. Fear of famine was not new, of course, and it is possible that those who moved did so because the soils in Wegbe were, in fact, better than what existed in Heve. Still, as noted, the fact that the famine came on the heels of such an unprecedented event like the earthquake was significant. Both events, the earthquake and the drought, were of enough concern that residents demanded explanations from the local priests. Their answers, however, were met with increasing skepticism. Some began to interpret the local priests' explanations as largely self-serving. When asked about the earthquake, for example, they had attributed it to the unwilling-ness of the missionaries to give to the gods the blue cloths that were worn only by the priests as a symbol of their profession. This skepticism emerged in a most public way in January 1863. Just six months after the earthquake and famine had hit the area, Heve's well-known local priest, Tenu Kwami, decided to convert to Christianity. He did so, in part, because of the dismay and disgust he felt over how the religious concerns of his fellow Ho citizens were being handled. Accord-ing to Tenu, his former fellow priests made far too many financial demands on those who came to them for spiritual assistance. He had experienced this him-self. Years earlier, when Tenu discovered that he was being spiritually called to become the priest of a local god, he found the demands were many. Even before his installation, he had to pay twelve strings of cowries to the priests and elders of his community. Over the next year, the demands rose exponentially to include a total of eighty-four strings and twenty-two heads of cowries, seven chickens (offered in lieu of the greater demand of a sheep), four additional chickens as well as large quantities of yams, fish, vegetables, and palm wine for the culminating ceremony. After all this, he still found he was not protected from harm by his god.[31] In one incident, when he was presumably under the spiritual control of the god, he almost died. We cannot know all the reasons Tenu Kwami chose to convert to Christianity after serving his own god for many years. But, certainly, the financial demands that his fellow priests made on those who came to consult them, and their simultaneous inability to address effectively the peoples' many spiritual concerns, must have been a factor. He converted to Christianity. Others did not go that far, at least not yet. But skepticism did increase. For even if most continued to believe in the power of their gods, they began to question the trust-worthiness of the priests who were tasked with communicating with the deities on their behalf.[32]

In the fall of 1863, just two years after the earthquake and nine months after Tenu Kwami's conversion, Ho's political leader, Fia Motey Kofi, demonstrated his own concerns about the extent to which the pronouncements of some of the local priests should be taken seriously. As frequently happened every fall, many fell ill and died. 1863 was no different. But when a seemingly quite healthy and very well-respected man from Wegbe unexpectedly passed away, and when many others succumbed as well, some found it difficult to accept that these deaths were the result of natural causes. Instead, a woman—through whom a god was believed to have spoken when it possessed her—blamed the missionaries. According to this god, the Europeans had dug a pit (intended to eventually become a well), into which the souls of those who would later die had fallen. That was what had killed them. Only if the hole was filled would death spare others in Wegbe. Fia Motey Kofi was strongly encouraged by his people to force the missionaries to fill the pit. A local priest from outside of Ho was also summoned to help secure spiritu-ally the well-being of the community. Neither Fia Kofi nor the priest, however, found the explanation for the deaths to be convincing. As noted by missionary Christian Hornberger, "the king found a way out [of this situation] . . . by letting us know that we should build a small enclosure around the pit so that no one could see inside," while the foreign priest simply mocked the people by saying: "What were [you] thinking . . . ? Whether [or not the missionaries] dig a pit on their land has nothing to do with any fetish!"[33]

Opportunities for skepticism increased even further in 1865. In that year, three years after the earthquake and two years after the famine, smallpox struck Ho.[34] Despite the efforts of the local priests to appease the deity that was associ-ated with using this disease to demonstrate its power, despite the peoples' efforts to clean their towns and quarantine the sick, many died.[35] At the same time, the people of Ho began to see the Christian missionaries and their god heal in ways that the traditional priests and their gods could not.[36] It happened in 1866 in Wegbe. A young boy from the town who attended the missionary school was bitten at the school by a snake. Frightened, the boy rushed home to his parents without telling his teacher. The missionaries only heard about it three hours later, at which point Johannes Vögelin, one of the missionaries who had medical training, went to find the boy, only to discover that a local priest had already begun treatment. His help was immediately rebuffed. The boy's parents were prepared to trust only the power of the local god and its priest to save their son. Two days later the missionaries heard the boy had died. When they went to offer their condolences, however, they discovered that the boy had not died after all, but rather was on his deathbed. It was at that point that the missionaries decided to act. After they returned to the mission station, another of the medically trained missionaries, Gottlob Zündel, went back to town on his own and treated the boy for two days. As he noted in a subsequent report about the incident, the results were positive in more ways than one:

> I tried to stop his cramps with medicine and treated him for a couple of days. To my great delight the boy is recovering and can be regarded as saved. God did this; we have to thank him. If the boy had died, the people would have said the fact that he was bitten on our territory was a sign of the fetish's annoyance about the boy visiting our school. Now they can see that the fetish did not help. . . . Not a day goes by without four to six people looking [to us] for . . . medical treatment.[37]

Zündel's success, and the positive impression it made on the people of Ho did not shake the faith that the vast majority in Ho placed in their own gods, however. For even missionary Hornberger (who had been so eager to insist that one could only make sense of the earthquake, and know how to operate properly in the world, more generally, through knowledge and acceptance of Christianity) acknowledged that the medical practices of local priests could be quite effective in treating a range of illnesses.[38] Thus, while the missionaries' own success in saving the boy's life did not go unnoticed, most, including Yawo, continued to seek treatment from the local priests and to believe in the local gods. All this was to be upended beginning in 1869. In that year, a devastating war engulfed Ho and the entire Krepi region.

The War Years and Their Aftermath

Although the peoples of the Krepi district had successfully freed themselves of Akwamu and Asante rule by the 1830s, neither of these powers was prepared to abandon its interests in the region. The polity of Anlo, which had long aligned itself with these states, felt the same way. Akwamu had gained great wealth from its dominance of the region. Its failure to find alternative sources of income elsewhere after it lost control of Krepi, however, led it to look again at reconquest. Asante's interests were somewhat different. It had also conquered sections of the Krepi district in the eighteenth century, but it lost control of those areas by 1818.[39] Thereafter, it relied on its ally, Akwamu, to secure its interests in the region. Those interests involved their need for security on the trade routes that passed through Krepi to the coastal areas east of the Volta River. For it was these routes that Asante used to bypass Britain's ban on the export of slaves from the ports west of the Volta. And it was on these roads that Asante obtained in exchange for its slave exports, the local salt, and European gunpowder and firearms that it needed to maintain its empire. Attacks on traders using these roads had increased since Akwamu lost control of the region. Asante found this intolerable.[40] Anlo, too, found its economic interests in the region threatened. Having long maintained a monopoly on European goods marketed in Ho and elsewhere, many in this coastal polity found by the early 1860s that the presence of the NDMG missionaries in the interior "was making the people [there] smarter than was good for Anlo's business." Profits had declined substantially.[41] But new opportunities existed as well. If Asante and Akwamu could reconquer Krepi, Anlo businessmen would certainly be among the beneficiaries. Anlo's traders could supply the firearms and gunpowder that Asante and Akwamu would need to carry out the war, as they had done many times in the past.[42] And if Anlo also participated in the war, success could bring into the polity, large numbers of enslaved prisoners who could be used to expand local businesses at a time when the slave trade even in the Anlo area was ending and the demand in Europe for local agricultural produce, especially palm oil, cotton, and rubber, brought the need for additional labor.[43] By 1867 all these overlapping interests led Asante, Akwamu, and Anlo to declare war on Krepi.

The invasion began in late May 1869, but the war did not reach Ho until 27 June. On that day, facing a combined force of Akwamu, Asante, and Anlo troops, the Ho military engaged the enemy. This was then followed by a quick retreat. They fled with their women and children to the east, to the neighboring polity of Takla, where they regrouped before retreating again further east to Agotime. There they engaged their enemy in a massive battle in August of 1869. Although they inflicted serious damage on the invading forces, they were again on the losing end of the conflict.[44] They retreated yet again, this time to the northeast, to the town of Atikpui, where they stayed briefly before moving on to Tove and Klonu. There they foisted themselves on a population that had no interest in being drawn into the war. Deeply afraid of the Asantes, the political leaders in both towns tried to persuade Ho's political leader, Fia Motey Kofi, to capitulate. Kofi refused. Instead, he remained in the area for three months, before moving again to Yokele. Here, other towns joined Ho and Agotime to battle their common enemies, but again they were forced to retreat.[45] This, in fact, characterized Ho's approach to the war: confront, retreat; confront, retreat. Faced with a superior number of enemy fighters, they dared not engage in sustained battle. Rather, they resorted to guerilla tactics, harassing and then scattering. Still, the toll that the war took on the people of Ho was heavy. For after leaving Yokele, they were forced to move on foot fourteen more times, over about one hundred thirty-two kilometers within a span of about six months. Not all citizens of Ho, however, followed their troops as they fought and retreated across the region. Some sought refuge in those communities in which they had already established deep connections. A few children, for example, instead of remaining with their Ho fathers, accompanied their mothers to the villages of their maternal relatives. Those who fled to the polity of Taviefe, however, were in for a nasty surprise. Taviefe had decided to align itself with Asante, Akwamu, and Anlo. Thus, when they arrived, the children were promptly forcibly removed from their mothers' protective care and handed over to the Asantes to be killed or enslaved. Other towns did the same thing. The people of Ho found themselves hunted wherever they went, either by the invading forces and their local allies, or by those who sought to stay neutral by keeping out, by force if necessary, the refugees who flooded their towns.[46]

Hunger was ever present. Having been forced out of Ho in July of 1869, the town's residents had to abandon their fields before their staple crop, the yam, was ready to harvest.[47] They carried only what they could grab quickly. And when these stores were depleted, they had to buy, beg, borrow, or steal what they could from the communities through which they passed. In the towns where they were less than welcome, they had to depend on reluctant hosts to house and feed them. And in towns that willingly gave them temporary refuge, they often found themselves "taken advantage of, forced to pay higher prices for food than others paid, fined for every minor or imagined infraction."[48] When they did finally return to the Ho area in April 1870, having already suffered indebtedness and the loss of many to warfare, enslavement, disease, and starvation,[49] they met only devastation. Their homes had been thoroughly looted. All their clothing, money, firewood, mats, food, and anything made of iron, even their cooking pots, were gone. Their houses had been set on fire, their farms destroyed.[50] A return in April meant there was time to begin a new agricultural season, but they would still need immediate sustenance between April and December when the crops would be ready to be harvested. Many families were forced to sell or pawn their own relatives in order to buy food and make ends meet. NDMG missionary Johannes Merz described the situation that had emerged in the region as early as 1871 when the war had just ended:

> The times are still very difficult for the people. Most of them have amassed so much debt that one or more members of their families have been taken away

from them and sold. One man was prepared to give me three children if I would [only] lend him a little money. His mother, an old woman, had already been taken from him and sold. . . . People would very much like to buy back their pawned children, but the debts pile up year after year so that it ultimately becomes completely impossible for them do so.[51]

Food and fiscal difficulties were compounded by ongoing concerns about physical safety. In 1873, two years after the war ended, the people of Ho continued to live in very rude huts, constructed hastily and easily abandoned because of fear that those in the region against whom they had fought in the war—the polities of Taviefe and Adaklu, for example—might seek revenge for the losses they suffered.[52] Life was difficult indeed.

Yawo of Ho-Kpenoe was among the many who experienced much suffering. During the war, he successfully sought refuge in his mother's home polity of Taviefe. Somehow, he was able to persuade the leaders there, who had politically and militarily joined forces with Asante against the people of Ho, to refrain from handing him over to the Asantes to be killed or enslaved.[53] But neither he nor the Taviefes were able to escape the twists and turns in the war that was bringing such devastating consequences to so many. The Asantes moved one of their camps into Taviefe because of its easily defended mountain location. While there, though, they behaved as if they were in enemy territory. They used their military presence to take advantage of the population. One set of incidents made a particularly strong impression on the Taviefes who were still discussing it many years after the war ended. When Asante troops would relax in town, they would at times address those who passed by: "Say, you consider yourselves our friends and our allies? Do you understand our language?" to which they always got a melancholic "No" in reply. And when they were asked by the Asantes, "Do you understand the Ho and the Peki, when they speak?"; they had to reply with a "Yes." The Asantes would then respond, "And so you are not Asante but Krepi. And we have come here to fight you people! One can, therefore, not talk about alliance and friendship between us and you." At other times they shifted from dark, suggestive talk to ruses to cover their confiscation of property. This, too, was recalled with bitterness:

One day the drums sounded, whereupon the inhabitants of Taviefe assembled on the street. A respectable officer of the Asante started his speech by asking the people assembled, why they were so ill clad. "Now," he continued, "you have no cause to mourn; you should be happy! Don't you know that your big friends are in your midst?" After this speech everyone went home happy. They put on their most beautiful clothes and those who could, paraded about in sandals. The rejoicing might have lasted a week, and then the usual drums resounded in their ears. When they gathered together on the street, the same officer addressed them once again, now with a serious tone: "For a few days now I see you prancing daily in festive attire. You are not concerned about the fact that the great military commander, Netsui [i.e., Nantwi] is involved in a serious war? You are not friends, but enemies of the Asante!" . . . The goal he attained by this move . . . [was] to discover who were the richest . . . [so he could then] impose heavy monetary sentences on them.[54]

Acts of intimidation and tricks to strip the Taviefes of their most valued possessions were only the beginning salvos in a campaign of ruthless exploitation that the Asantes waged against their supposed allies. They looted their farms, leaving virtually nothing for the Taviefes themselves to eat. Then, the Asante military commander ordered the enslavement of as many Taviefe men, women, and children as his soldiers could capture to compensate for the otherwise dismal results of his campaign in Krepi.[55] Fear, starvation, loss of property, and the enslavement of friends and relatives is what Yawo experienced as a refugee in Taviefe. When the Asantes finally left the area, he, like others, found that they had lost everything. His house in Ho-Kpenoe was destroyed; all the material possessions he had accumulated were gone. Every indication that he had once been a very wealthy individual had vanished. He only managed to keep his household intact. That, in itself, was remarkable. By his side, still, were his three wives and his slaves. But the loss of everything else was an especially bitter blow to a man who had spent his entire adult life focusing on accumulating all that would gain him respect, even awe from his fellow Ho citizens. More devastating events were to come.

In early 1872 Yawo's older brother, Gamo, passed away after a long illness. Yawo described this tragedy as the final blow. Despite the fiscally difficult times, he had not "withheld any money" as he went from one local priest to another seeking treatment for his brother. None were helpful; no one could address whatever health issues his brother was facing. In the end, he died.[56] Adhering to the logic that was an integral part of the local religious system, Yawo believed that the gods had rejected the many sacrifices. They refused to save Gamo's life. More importantly, as Yawo reflected on the events of the past ten years, he came to believe that the local priests had either misled the people, or the gods were simply not as powerful as he had believed them to be. In 1862, when an unprecedented earthquake shook the entire region, the priests could only offer an explanation which required the NDMG missionaries in Wegbe to provide them with material goods for their own personal use. The earthquake was then followed in quick succession by crop failures in late 1862, the outbreak of a smallpox epidemic in 1865, and the 1869–71 war that devastated the area and left in its wake years of misery. Despite prayers and sacrifices, the gods had prevented none of these events.

Prior to the death of his brother, Yawo was, of course, aware of the string of disasters that had hit Ho, but he gave no serious thought to the notion that the gods could not be appeased or that they had, for some reason, forsaken the polity. Even when the war came on the heels of the earthquake and the smallpox epidemic, he held steadfastly to his religion. He continued to rely—as did the vast majority of Ho citizens—on the protection that he thought would be forthcoming from the local deities as well as the talismans he and others had purchased for protection.[57] It was the death of his older brother that prompted him to reassess. He began to recall the many disasters that preceded the war; he considered the ongoing struggles that followed it. And he remembered the speech that the missionary, Christian Hornberger, had made at the gathering that the Ho political leader, Fia Motey Kofi, had called immediately after the quake. In that speech, Hornberger had expressed no shock at the existence of earthquakes. He was very familiar with them. More importantly, he had predicted more disasters to come: "stronger earthquakes, terrible hard times."[58] None of the local priests had made such prognostications. More importantly, the Christian missionary's pronouncements seem to have come true. Yawo began to question. Why had he not taken more seriously what the missionaries had to say? They came regularly to his hometown of Kpenoe to preach, and they did so largely because Gamo, his older brother, had expressed his eagerness to hear what they had to say. It was, in fact, Gamo who had invited them to Kpenoe in the first place. In addition, Yawo knew that Gamo was not alone in his questioning. Others in his town had not only expressed doubts about the local gods, but had gone even further and converted to Christianity. One such person, as noted, was the particularly influential priest, Tenu Kwami, Yawo's neighbor. Tenu had been disquieted by the constant financial demands that his fellow local religious leaders made on the people. Too many demanded money for every small service they provided. In addition, the god that he himself had served as priest, had placed such onerous, seemingly impossible demands on him that he felt the need to free himself from its clutches. In January 1863, he converted to Christianity, taking the name Samuel, and in 1865, after living in Heve, he moved back to his and Yawo's hometown, Kpenoe. When the war came in 1867, he made it very clear that he had no intention of following local custom. He refused to participate in the offering of prayers and sacrifices to the gods; he did not use amulets to protect himself and his family. He put his faith, instead, in the Christian God.

Yawo was well aware of Samuel's stance. As the war approached, he may even have participated in ridiculing Tenu for the position he took. For many in Kpenoe were afraid that his refusal to join in their rituals could threaten them all by angering the very gods they hoped would protect them.[59] Only after the end of the war, and only after his brother's death did Yawo reconsider his views about the power of the Christian God in which Samuel Tenu had placed his faith. Why did so many people who adhered to all the beliefs and practices outlined by the local priests lose so many relatives to enslavement and death during the war, yet

Samuel and his family seemed to have escaped such horrors? During the battle between Ho and Asante at Agotime, one of his children had been taken captive by the enemy along with so many others. The next day, however, Samuel heard his child call to him. By some miracle, and much to his surprise and joy, his little one had escaped.[60] Knowing of this incident, Yawo must have asked himself, could this mean that the Christian God was more powerful than the local deities?[61] He was not prepared to answer this question during the war or immediately after. But with the death of his brother, it was one he could no longer avoid. Over a period of just ten years, too many unexplained, frightening events and tragedies had occurred. He wondered if his relentless pursuit of wealth, his desire for multiple wives, had led to all the tragedies he had experienced. The Christian missionaries who had spent time with his elder brother had preached against the practice of polygyny, but they were not alone in expressing their disdain for this practice. So, too, did some Ho locals, most often during heated quarrels when their emotions overwhelmed their socialization to show respect to those with money and power.[62] As noted by missionary Jakob Spieth, "the most devastating opinion[s] of the natives come to light occasionally in quarrels, in which, say, a monogamist calls out to his polygamous neighbor: 'I have only one wife and am not a debaucher that hoards many wives at home!'" Did this local subaltern condemnation of excess, prompted largely perhaps by jealousy and given focus by missionary opprobrium, bring him to reassess what he now began to think was his past inordinate focus on accumulation? In his own statement to the missionaries, Yawo indicated that he had spent "his entire life striving for riches and pleasure," yet he had lost everything: his house, his brother, his faith in the local gods. He felt forlorn, totally lost. "He longed for true happiness."[63] It was in this state of mind that he turned to Christianity.

In opening himself to this new religion, Yawo recalled the Christian messages he had heard in Wegbe and at his brother Gamo's house. He listened to the missionaries who had returned to Ho after the war in 1871.[64] And this time, their words resonated with him in ways they had not before. He remembered Hornberger's prediction of coming disasters; that the earthquake was a sign that the people should awaken from their slumber to begin a new life.[65] He heard missionary assistant Aaron Onyipayede state that: "whoever went with Jesus could only but expect that storms would come; yet it was [also] certain . . . [that] no storm could hurt us . . . no affliction or persecution would tear us from God's love. [And] "if they take from us our possessions, our honor, our child and wife, let them go [Psalm 46] . . . for the promise of eternal life surely remains ours; and that is certainly worth much more than all the sorrows of this time."[66] Yawo recalled, he listened, he heard. In November 1872 he made his decision. He would study the new faith with his friend and neighbor, former local priest Samuel Tenu Kwami. And in December of that same year, he also decided to brave the highwaymen-infested roads in the still unsettled region and travel with Samuel on foot to the missionary station in Waya, ten hours away. There, he declared his interest in Christianity and received over a period of two weeks his first set of lessons in the new faith. On returning to Kpenoe, he continued his studies. By that time, Aaron Onyipayede had begun to travel again to Ho on behalf of the European missionaries to renew their work there. Among those who came to him for further instruction during his periodic visits was Yawo. Onyipayede, with the assistance of Samuel Tenu, taught him "all that [was] necessary for the salvation of a Christian: the Ten Commandments, the Lord's Prayer and the universal Christian creed." In July 1873 he traveled to Waya again for three more months of instruction. On 28 September 1873, he and another relative who had taken this journey with him, were finally baptized and participated in their first communion. From that day he took the name Noah Yawo.[67]

Converting to Christianity was no easy task. Not only did it require a lengthy period of study, acceptance of a very different doctrine, and adherence to totally new norms as to how one should conduct oneself in the world,[68] Noah Yawo also had to withstand the slings and arrows of his relatives, friends, and neighbors. They were not happy. His mother traveled from Taviefe to Kpenoe to express her serious disapproval. His children were displeased as well. His neighbors mocked him, calling Noah and the other Christians "Ayesutowo," those who belong to Christ. They accused them of being lazy for not working on Sunday. They derided them as rootless bums for traveling so frequently to Waya. In addition, they blamed Noah Yawo and anyone else who expressed interest in converting for so angering the gods that the entire community was being punished with poor harvests.[69] Especially irritating to the Kpenoe citizens was the fact that Yawo, Samuel Tenu Kwami, and Mose Dake, Yawo's relative who had been baptized with him, refused to participate in local funerals or to have their sick children cared for by the local priests. Funerary rituals became a particularly sore point between the local Christians and their polytheistic neighbors. Local custom demanded that guns be fired to announce the death of an individual and that they be fired again after the body had been prepared for burial. Public displays of grief were expected as well. Family members were supposed to show the depth of their sadness by engaging in open weeping and the singing of dirges. The deceased's companions would play commemorative music that most often involved—in the opinion of the European missionaries—incessant singing, drumming, dancing, and the sharing of alcohol.[70] None of this was deemed acceptable according to the Christian customs introduced by the missionaries. Funerals, instead, were to be solemn affairs. Emotions were to be kept in check. Only Christian hymns were to be sung; only biblical recitations and quiet prayers were to be offered. When Noah Yawo and the other Christians refused to participate in the local customs, when the Christian men, in particular, refused to fire their guns to honor the dead, the local people were outraged.[71] How could they refuse to do this? Equally strong emotions developed when Christian fathers ignored the pleadings of their polytheistic wives and in-laws and prohibited them from consulting local priests when their children were sick. If the child died, relations could get particularly ugly, as noted by missionary assistant Josef Reindorf:

> To[ward] the end of November '76, one Christian in Axlixa [i.e., Ahliha, one of the Ho towns] . . . Gottlob Kwasi, had been in a great perplexity with the death of a grown up daughter of his. It came that the daughter got sick. . . . The father would not comply with the request of the mother and grandmother to let them apply fetishes to the sick daughter, but rather did apply European medicine. . . . [He did so until] he was so strongly constrained and forced by the grandmother [that he let] the girl [be attended to by the fetish priest]. He could not help than to let the girl [go]. But . . . one Sunday, . . . the grandmother and the grandfather [went] to consult [an] oracle for the girl, . . . [and] Gottlob [had] also got up [to go to] the [church] service. . . . Just after the service, it was said that the child is dead. . . .Then the people lifted up their voices lamenting the girl, saying that Gottlob is the murderer of his daughter. . . . On the morrow [i.e., the next day], the kings and the elders of the place gathered together about the matter . . . and we [too] . . . set ourselves before them. They said different things against Gottlob and the other Christians, and [they] laid false charges upon Gottlob that he [was] the cause that his daughter died because he [at] first refused to let [the priests] apply fetishes to her and he was then away to church whilst his own daughter [was] in [the] pangs of death.[72]

Nothing seems to have ultimately come of the charges against Gottlob, but other incidents did result in the leveling of serious sanctions against both Yawo and his fellow Christians in Kpenoe.

In October 1875, Kpenoe saw its first set of couples participate in a Christian marriage ceremony. Noah Yawo took as his only wife the recently baptized Lydia;[73] Noah's relative, Mose Dake, married Hanna, who like Lydia had also just been baptized the day before, and Mose's friend Isaak Kwami took as his wife, Salome. Their happiness in joining together as Christian couples was shattered all too soon, however. Isaac Kwami's wife died suddenly, shortly after they were married, and then in a hunting accident in December of that same year, Isaak accidently shot and killed Mose Dake. If these tragedies were not enough, Isaak, as well as the entire Christian community, was then prosecuted for the accidental death of Mose. According to the local laws in force at the time:

> Whoever kills someone deliberately or inadvertently is usually sold and the whole family of the culprit becomes indebted. If the culprit is to be killed, that can only happen if he is handed over to the blood avengers by one of his close relatives, usually the uncle. However, if the uncle, in agreement with the family, does not surrender the culprit, the family that takes vengeance has

permission to recover its losses by snatching away and selling family members of the culprit and destroying their homes and farms. If a person who has exposed himself to blood vengeance quickly flees, he himself is certain of never going back home. . . . However his family has to pay all expenses incurred and to see to the cleansing of the defiled land. Failing to do that will make the land lose its fertility.[74]

As a citizen of Kpenoe, Isaak was subject to this law. Equally serious, the father of the deceased was deeply antagonistic toward the growing Christian community in Kpenoe. So when Isaak was put on trial for accidentally killing Mose Dake, Mose's father sought to have him given as great a punishment as possible. He was sentenced to enslavement, while his family was levied a heavy fine.[75] Only because the European missionaries and his fellow converts managed to intervene was the sentence not carried out as issued. Instead, the missionary Johannes Illg managed to obtain his freedom and then relocated him permanently to Waya, while his fellow Kpenoe Christians took responsibility for paying the fines that had been levied on his family. This did not end their difficulties, however. Animosity toward the converts had been growing for some time. Some families were so opposed to the new religion that they insisted that their daughters divorce any men who wished to convert.[76] Others cursed their children if they showed interest in the new religion.[77] So, when Isaak accidently shot and killed Mose Dake, the political leaders in Kpenoe used this tragedy as opportunity to sanction the entire Christian community. They banned the converts for an unspecified period of time from drawing water from local sources, forbade them to sing their Christian songs in public, and prohibited them from traveling to the other Ho towns to attend worship services. Experiencing the hostility of his family, friends, and neighbors was quite difficult for Yawo. Only with the support of Samuel Tenu Kwami was he able to resist feeling completely overwhelmed.[78] Samuel counseled patience, and it appears Noah Yawo followed that advice. He remained faithful to his new religion.[79] With time, more people in Kpenoe converted, and this in turn provided Noah with a larger community from which to draw strength. He would certainly need the support of this community, for additional challenges lay ahead.

Faith and Finances

When Noah first expressed interest in Christianity in 1872, he had still not recovered from the devastation wrought by the war. He and the members of his household, like other Kpenoe residents, were frequently hungry. And his ability to market his goods and engage in trade more generally was severely hindered by the continued unsettled conditions in the region. Highway robbers plagued many of the roads. For while Asante, Akwamu, and Anlo had withdrawn from the area, they left in their wake many neighboring communities like Ho and Ta-viefe that had fought on different sides in the war and whose citizens were now seeking to wreak havoc on those who had harmed them. Travel was extremely hazardous and remained so until the 1880s.[80] During the war, Yawo had managed to keep safe and by his side, both his wives and his slaves. It was with their emotional support and their labor that Yawo would begin rebuilding his life. Yet his conversion to Christianity seemed to threaten all of this. Polygyny was not allowed for Christian converts. If someone had multiple wives, they were required to divorce all but one before they were baptized. Yawo accepted this rule. He ended his marriage to two of his wives and remained married to the third, Lydia, only after she agreed to convert. At his baptism, he also agreed not to purchase any new slaves, to free the children of the slaves he currently owned, and to give his adult slaves the opportunity to obtain their freedom.[81]

This would have been a very significant step for anyone in West Africa during this time. Having multiple wives as well as slaves significantly enhanced one's productive and marketing capacities relative to those who had only one wife and no slaves. In Ho, wives, slaves, and the older children of both were given land on which to produce the vegetables (beans, pepper, okra, tomatoes, groundnuts, maize, etc.) that provided a significant portion of the food consumed by the household. They also grew a few yams and oil palms, to supplement the much larger quantity of yams and oil palms for which husbands were responsible. A portion of any surplus was stored for future consumption, while the rest was sold in markets in the area. A large household could produce a great deal and reap significant profits if the harvest was good, and if its members also had excellent marketing skills. The money earned could then be invested in additional labor (slaves, debt pawns, and wives) and livestock (sheep and goats) as well as in consumer goods (expensive cloth and beads) that were displayed at public gatherings where wealthy husbands would be quite liberal in their sharing of both food and palm wine. Such men were also able to build and maintain large houses that included plenty of rooms to entertain guests.

Wealth brought respect and influence. Yet Yawo agreed to give up so many of his assets upon his conversion. Why did he do it? How did he do it? We know little about his wives. It is unclear, for example, where they came from or what their status was. We only know that the two wives he divorced agreed to remarry men in Yawo's extended family. Their decisions meant that the labor they had provided, while lost to Yawo, could continue to benefit his extended family. We do know something about his third wife. This was the woman who decided to remain with Noah and then took the name Lydia after she converted to Christianity. Her decision, however, was not free of coercion. Noah had inherited her as a wife from his older brother, Gamo, who had acquired her as a slave. She had no relatives in the area, and would have had no place to go if neither Noah nor his extended family wanted her. Even if she were able to find a place of refuge, she would have had to get there on roads that were terribly unsafe. In fact, her enslavement came as a result of her decision to travel with others from her hometown of Taviefe to find food in Adaklu, some 19 kilometers to the south. On that journey, she and her traveling companions were attacked and enslaved. Once she became the slave/wife of Gamo and then later Yawo, leaving was not a realistic option for someone who had no family and nowhere else to go. If she had decided to leave him—as he demanded if she did not convert—and had agreed to marry someone else in his family, as had Yawo's other wives, she had no relatives to make sure that she would not simply be sold if her new husband was forced to sell her because of the kinds of economic difficulties that plagued everyone in the region. Did Yawo know this when he issued the ultimatum that she convert to Christianity? He must have. Given these circumstances, we must ask again, how much did he really sacrifice when he agreed to convert? Was it as difficult as one might think for him to give up his wives when he could arrange for his extended family to gain two additional members at a time when so many had lost family members to the war just two years earlier? How difficult was it for him when he knew himself that he would probably continue to benefit from having a spouse who had no relatives to visit, no family to defend her interests, and who had every reason to do anything he asked of her? Yawo was a farmer, but he was also a businessman. As noted, his willingness to seize new opportunities, and his tendency to embrace fully, and with a certain degree of single-mindedness, the tasks he set for himself made him the wealthy man he had become by about 1860. He lost a great deal in the war. But he was also determined to recover as much as he could as quickly as possible. Accepting Christianity squared with his desire to associate with a god that was more powerful than the local deities (whose priests had not only demanded what little money he had, but then failed to save his much-beloved older brother).[82] But it also meant managing the requirements of his new faith in ways that would allow him to at least maintain a respectable position within his own community. One way to do that was to accept the need to have only one wife, but to handle this change in a way that minimized the damage both to himself and his family. He did the same with regard to the management of his slaves.

Immediately after the war, but prior to his conversion, Yawo sought to soften his difficult economic situation by collecting on a number of outstanding loans. Doing so could prove to be quite difficult, however. Sometime prior to 1869, Yawo had lent two hundred fifty shillings to a man from Kpando. With the outbreak of the war, the borrower fled to Akuapem, making it impossible for Yawo to recover his money. By the end of the war, however, as mentioned, Yawo was in dire financial straits. He decided to act. First, he located a woman and child in Peki who came from Kpando, the same hometown as the borrower. Yawo then organized a group of men who traveled to Peki where the woman and child were living. They kidnapped both and handed them over to Yawo, who then promptly sold the two as slaves to a buyer in Agotime. In this way he recovered the money he had lent to the Kpando man. This all occurred between 1871 and 1872, before his conversion. By 1873 Noah had become a Christian. He had also agreed to no longer engage in these kinds of practices. Though it was considered the standard method locally for recovering a bad loan, all converts were forbidden to engage in debt bondage, a practice the European missionaries considered to be a form of slavery. So, when Noah Yawo was approached by a Peki man who accused him of kidnapping a women and a child that belonged to him, he felt obliged by his faith to acknowledge his actions. The Peki man informed Noah that the woman and child were not members of his family. Rather, they were his own debt pawns whom he had received as security for a loan he had given to a man from Agotime. Yawo's kidnapping of the two people put him in a very difficult situation. If the Agotime man came to him to repay the loan, he would be unable to return the woman and child. The Peki man then demanded that Noah get back the woman and child from the person to whom he had sold them. It was at this point that serious negotiations began. The Peki man wanted Yawo to retrieve the woman and child and insisted that, as a guarantee, Noah provide to Kwadjo De, the political leader of Peki, two people who would remain with him until Noah returned with the two kidnap victims. In making this demand, the Peki man was acutely aware of the loss of labor he had suffered because of Yawo's actions. Debt pawns were incorporated into the household of the lender where they worked for the lender. This labor—provided without compensation—constituted the interest payment on the loan that had been given to the borrower. In losing his pawns, the Peki man not only lost his ability to demand repayment from the borrower, but he also lost the interest payments. Noah had his own concerns, however. The woman and child he had sold to recover his own bad loan may have already been sold several times to different buyers, making it difficult if not impossible to find them. Eventually, however, Noah and the Peki man successfully negotiated a compromise. Noah agreed to find the woman and child, but he would provide only one person as security. Noah then traveled to Agotime. Luckily for him, the two kidnap victims had not been sold, but the man who had bought them from Yawo refused to sell them back to him. What to do now? Noah returned to Peki and offered to compensate the Peki lender by paying him the same amount that he had lent to the person who had given him the woman and child as security. In this way, at least the Peki man would have his loan repaid. The Peki man, however, refused this offer. Instead, he demanded twice the amount, £11 instead of £5.5. It is unclear why he doubled the amount. Perhaps he was adding to the loan the amount he had lost when the woman and child were removed from his custody and were thus no longer able to work for him. Whatever the case, Noah agreed to pay the higher fee.

He did not have the money, however. It is at this point that he turned to the missionaries. In 1875 Noah requested and received a grant of £6 from the European missionaries. But when he returned to Peki to pay the agreed amount (with the remaining £5 to be paid later), he was dragged into court by both the Peki lender and the borrower (who had suddenly surfaced in town). In the end, he was forced to agree to pay 366 shillings, a little over £18. This was more than one and half times the £11 originally agreed upon, and three times the amount he had received from the European missionaries. This left Noah deeply in debt. Again, he turned to the missionaries. This time they organized a raffle in which bidders paid a fee in hopes of winning an expensive cloth that Noah had donated. The missionaries also brought his plight to the attention of congregations in Germany that were supportive of the NDMG. This resulted in Noah receiving a number of donated items from Hamburg. At the same time, he redoubled his own efforts to find the many borrowers to whom he had given loans before the war, but who were now in default. By early 1876 these efforts had allowed him to substantially reduce his debt and to build a quite large home with the kinds of amenities associated only with European houses.[83] Noah was back on his feet.

Throughout this period, when he was quite impoverished, but working to improve his financial standing, Noah refused to relinquish his slaves. He could have sold them since there was a thriving market in the region for able men, women, and children; or he could have freed them as he had promised in 1873 when he was baptized. But he did not. Technically, he was under no obligation to do so. In 1877 Ho had not been colonized by any European power, and even if it had, rarely did colonial authorities implement with vigor their own laws outlawing slavery. The Christian missionary society with which Noah was affiliated, the NDMG, had banned slaveholding, but only for its African teachers and catechists. The prohibition did not apply to ordinary members of the African Christian congregations like Noah. Converts were instead simply encouraged to free their enslaved children, to give them a Christian education, and to allow the adults they owned to buy their freedom. The scriptural rationale for this, outlined by the head of the NDMG, Michael Zahn, was that "'Thou shall not keep any slaves' is not a commandment." But there were practical considerations as well. Zahn was concerned that if the NDMG banned slave ownership, as had its sister missionary society the Basel Mission which operated on the Gold Coast,[84] "it might . . . lose the still small congregations that had been won only with great sacrifice."[85] Thus, with no scripture-based obligation to do otherwise, Noah kept his slaves and resisted pressures to free them. He complied only in 1877.[86] Why, and why then?

Noah was a devout Christian, but he also lived in the real world. From 1869 to the 1880s, that world was a very a difficult place. War, drought, and the threat of starvation were daily realities. Crop yields were unpredictable, and poor harvests not uncommon. Obtaining extra income by trading was severely limited by the continuing warfare that wracked the region after Asante, Akwamu, and Anlo withdrew. If Noah had freed his slaves after he converted to Christianity, this would have deprived him of the labor that was so essential to the production of his household's subsistence. These same household members could even try to produce a surplus to sell in the local markets while Noah worked to recover the monies he had lent to others before the war. Freeing his slaves immediately did not make economic sense. His refusal, however, did not mean that he wavered in his faith. Instead, he remained so faithful to the Christian God, so steady in his service to the NDMG that they could not help but support him economically when he was in distress.[87] Noah had become one of the leaders in the Kpenoe congregation, and an elder in his local church. He encouraged others to convert, and supported unequivocally the work of the African assistants and the European missionaries who worked in the area. Noah was also aware of the extent to which the NDMG would support members of its Christian community. Kpenoe's first Christian convert Tenu Kwami first encountered the NDMG missionaries in 1859 when they visited the Ho village of Heve where he was both a local priest and a debt slave. Initially, he was very hostile toward the missionaries, but the more he listened to their sermons, the more he became interested in what they had to say. Eventually, in late 1862, he and his master moved to Wegbe where he was invited to work for the missionaries and to learn carpentry. It was this invitation, issued because of his obvious interest in the new faith, that allowed Tenu Kwami to make enough money to free himself from servitude.[88] So, when Noah Yawo found himself in great financial difficulty in 1873, he knew he, too, could turn to the missionaries.

Yet another benefit that came to those, like Noah, who converted to Christianity was the economic connections they were able to make through the NDMG. Ever since they began working in the Krepi region in 1852, the NDMG had opened schools and seminaries with the hope of producing enough Christian teachers and catechists to supplement their efforts in spreading the new faith. Those who attended the schools beyond the usual six years (in which they were taught reading, writing, English, and mathematics, as well as a great deal about the Christian faith), were given in-depth instruction in the English language as well as business management. English was the language of business on the coast, and exposure to European business practices was considered essential for assistants, teachers, and catechists. All would have to handle the affairs of any new mission station to which they were assigned. This included working with the person at their station who bought locally produced goods to be transported to the coast and exported to Europe in exchange for the kinds of materials needed by the missionaries in the field. They also needed to be able to manage the workers who would be contracted to help build and maintain the station. All had to be paid from what little resources the stations could raise to supplement the limited support provided by the NDMG. Those who received this education and remained as employees of the NDMG often used their newly acquired business skills to engage in trade for themselves.[89] Prior to the war, the African assistants trained by the NDMG had shared their business knowledge with those in the interior with whom they had contact. This, in turn, had given the people of Krepi so much information about business on the coast that they were able to demand higher prices for their goods. After the war, when the missionaries returned to the interior and resumed their trade activities, they again provided the people of Ho with regular information about commodity prices as well as a market for their goods. This was quite a boon for Ho residents. Enmities caused by the war made travel to the coast quite unsafe.[90] These same enmities caused the political leader of Ho, Fia Motey Kofi, to prohibit traders from Anlo, Akwamu, Asante, and Taviefe (whose polities had militarily attacked Ho during the war) from conducting business in the area. This ban was lifted in 1884,[91] but, in the period between 1872 and 1884, the NDMG assistants, teachers, and catechists were among the few with contacts on the coast to whom the people of Ho could sell their palm oil, cotton, and rubber for export to Europe. Those who were willing to cultivate the new crops intro-duced by the missionaries—coffee and cocoa—found as well ready buyers among the missionary community's African employees. Knowing these individuals as fellow members of a small, embattled Christian community, provided Noah with the opportunity to resume a profitable trading career. This, in turn, helped Noah extricate himself from poverty.

   Why did Noah free his slaves and why did he do it when he did? Noah Yawo embraced Christianity fully, with the same degree of single-mindedness that he approached his financial affairs. The Christian God he embraced, after he was so bitterly disappointed by the local gods, preferred—he was told—that he give up not only two of his three wives, but also his slaves. As a faithful and devout Chris-tian, he did just that. But he also managed this request when it was economically feasible for him to do so. He freed his slaves and debt pawns only after success-fully recouping the many loans he had made before the war. He did not have to do this. Christianity, as interpreted by the NDMG, did not demand it of him. Yet, he did it anyway. Such was the seriousness with which he took his faith.

Legacies

Documenting Noah Yawo's legacy with regard to the issue of slavery is difficult. No family histories have been orally recorded and the German missionary re-cords that so carefully described his life and the service to his community fail to mention him after 1883. What we do know is that, by this date, Noah had been so successful in encouraging the other members of his household and a number of his fellow Kpenoe citizens to convert to Christianity that the NDMG decided to establish a permanent station in the town. Assigned to lead the Kpenoe Christians in worship and to coordinate educational services was Rudolph Mallet, the first African ordained by the NDMG to serve as a minister in his own right.[92] As a former slave himself, and a known vocal opponent of slavery, it is likely that Mallet encouraged Noah to use his position as an elder in the new congregation to convince others who were interested in converting and who were also slave owners to follow his own lead in freeing their slaves. Mallet certainly did this elsewhere in the region.[93] That slavery continued to be widely practiced in the area is clear, however, due, in part, to the nature of colonial rule.

In 1850, Britain claimed exclusive trading rights over the entire Krepi district after it purchased from Denmark the Keta fort and their claimed rights to be the sole European purchaser of goods that were produced both on the coast and in the interior. Periodically, Britain conducted political and military operations in the region when it felt its economic interests were threatened by opposition to its policies and by the local conflicts that could disrupt trade.[94] Overall, however, it's presence was very limited until 1874 when Britain extended the abolition of slavery to the region. Even then, it did little to stop slavery and the domestic slave trade. Between 1883 and 1895, competing claims by Britain, France, and Germany over who had territorial rights over the area became heated. Each supported exploratory expeditions and the signing of treaties with local rulers as they sought to ensure their exclusive access to the palm oil, cotton, and rubber that was being produced in the interior, and control over the routes on which goods from the Sudanic areas of West Africa passed to the Atlantic coast.[95] In 1890 Britain and Germany agreed to resolve at least one territorial question: who would control Ho and the rest of the Krepi district. The Heligoland Treaty stated that Germany would exercise that authority. Ho came under German jurisdiction. Colonial administration of the area came slowly, however. In 1885 Germany officially abolished slavery, but did virtually nothing to enforce the new law.[96] Only in 1899 did the colonial government establish its first outpost in Ho.[97] And even then, it did little to address the issue of slavery. It is true that slave ownership was not as extensive in Ho as it was on the coast or much further north in Kpando, Buem, and Keta Krachi.[98] Still, it existed, so when news that the German colonial government tolerated both slavery and the slave trade in Ho and throughout German Togoland, it created a scandal in Germany in the 1890s. Pressure from a concerned German public, however, did little. Bent on minimizing expenditures and maximizing profits from its colonial possessions, the government responded to its critics by attacking the credibility of those who exposed the situation. They embraced the notion that slavery in Africa was a benign institution and required no serious attention. They did nothing.[99] It was thus left to Noah Yawo and others like him, inspired by their Christian faith, to encourage or cajole other slave owners, particularly those within their own Christian communities, to give up their slaves.

Belief that slavery was an acceptable practice did end, if only slowly, as happened in most other parts of West Africa. Multiple factors explain this. That powerful colonial governments halted the many wars, small and large, that fueled the supply of slaves was important. So, too, was their official declaration that slavery and slave trading were now illegal, even if they did little to enforce the abolition. These measures, at a minimum, gave the formerly enslaved and former slave masters pause as they had to reevaluate the very institution that had defined their lives. Attitudes were further challenged from the late nineteenth century through the mid-1940s when the enslaved themselves took advantage of the changed economic climate to alter their situations. During this period, they were able to travel more freely, engage in wage labor, gain new skills, such as carpentry at missionary schools, and then market them where demand existed, and take advantage of shifting landholding patterns to lease or purchase property on which to grow their own cash crops.[100] Political developments in the 1920s, '30s, '40s, and '50s were also significant. African nationalist politicians protested the use of forced labor by colonial governments, equating the practice, and colonialism, in general, with slavery.[101] These developments were key to altering local attitudes. But important as well were the earlier actions of those like Noah and former slave Christian converts, like Rudolph Mallet, who took even more seriously than many of their Europeans counterparts the notion that slavery was not just illegal but unethical. Using Christian rhetoric, they reinforced old ideas already present in the local culture that acknowledged the suffering caused by slavery and the slave trade. But they also emphasized the notion that slavery was not merely illegal, but it was, and always had been, unethical, inhumane, and, for Christians, a sin.[102] In taking such a stance, Noah Yawo, as a respected and relatively wealthy member of his community, contributed in his own small way to the demise of the notion that slavery was a regrettable, but necessary and legitimate feature of everyday life.[103]

4 Concluding Thoughts

SCHOLARS HAVE LONG had an interest in exploring why those in positions of power make the decisions they do. Those who study the history of international affairs have analyzed the various factors that seem to have influenced the decisions of presidents, prime ministers, and dictators to avoid confrontations or to go to war. Legal scholars have examined the social, cultural, educational, and personal backgrounds of a number of U.S. Supreme Court justices to understand how they came to their decisions on important constitutional questions. The writers of biographies have explored as well the factors that appear to have influenced how a specific European or American slave owner managed his or her human property.[1] Of particular concern in this study has been the decision making of West African slave owners. How did they handle the abolition and why did they respond in the ways they did? Why did some choose to use violence to maintain the institution of slavery, while others accepted abolition and simply freed their slaves? Why did some incorporate the formerly enslaved into their families as kin, but then refuse to view them as equals, while others insisted that the newly freed be given the same kind of respect accorded the freeborn? What economic, political, and religious motives, what personal experiences and individual proclivities influenced how they handled abolition?

In constructing the biographies of three individuals who lived during the late nineteenth and early twentieth centuries in what is now southeastern Ghana, I have emphasized how different their responses were. Amegashie refused to accept abolition as the new law of the land. He sent armed men to attack former slaves who tried to return home; he relocated his own slaves to an area outside of British colonial jurisdiction. Placed on trial in the colonial courts for slave dealing, he refused to acknowledge either the unethical or illegal practice of slavery. Tamakloe, on the other hand, a man from the same community as Amegashie, followed a very different path. While he never formally freed his slaves, he gave them the kinds of opportunities and a degree of respect that eluded many in Anlo, even those who could claim to be of free descent. He made it possible for his former slaves to obtain Western education at a time when such training had become the key to social and economic mobility. He championed the official titling of the leaders of his three slave villages. Once they were recognized as village leaders, *hanuawo*, they were able to voice their opinions and participate as equals in the governing body that made decisions on behalf of the entire Anlo polity. Noah Yawo, a citizen of the polity of Ho, was a businessman like Amegashie and Tamakloe. He engaged in farming, but his wealth came largely from trading and moneylending. By 1867 he had the financial resources to buy slaves in the local market and to marry and maintain three wives. Six years later, however, in 1873, he made a commitment to give it all up. He vowed to free his slaves upon his conversion to Christianity, and, in 1877, he did just that. He freed his last slave. Amegashie, Tamakloe, and Yawo each took a different path. Yet their responses to abolition were similar.

All sought to preserve their economic and social status. Amegashie refused to give up his slaves. Tamakloe took a more nuanced approach, but one that also served his own political and economic interests as he shifted from slave owner to patron. Noah Yawo took the more radical step of freeing his slaves, but he did so only after securing financial stability. In deciding how to respond—to resist, take advantage of, or embrace abolition—all three were influenced by a desire to maintain their economic, social, and political status. But personal traits were also important. Amegashie was described in his lifetime as having a prickly personality. Highly conscious of his own status, he was acutely sensitive to any perceived lack of respect. He was also deeply invested in upholding established hierarchical standards. The abolition of slavery came at a time when he had managed to obtain great wealth (defined in part by the number of slaves he owned) and had also attained a respected position at the very top of his polity's political order. This he achieved despite his slave origins. His response to abolition was a reflection of the threat that abolition posed to his economic interests, but it was also a result of his personality. Unwilling to countenance this assault on all that he had achieved, he reacted violently, and unapologetically to abolition. Tamakloe also recognized the threat, but as someone who was an astute politician, able and willing to adjust as circumstances demanded, he pursued other opportunities made available by the changing climate to retain his social, political, and economic status. He invested in mining, timber, and agricultural products that were in demand in Europe, as well as in the education of the most promising young people whose new skills could be marshaled in support of his business interests. But it was his sensitivity to the social stigma felt deeply by those of slave descent that also contributed to his decision to embrace the ethical aspects of abolition by incorporating his former slaves as equally valued and respected members of his extended family and his polity's political system. Noah Yawo responded to the recommendation of his Christian mentors to free his slaves because he, too, managed to establish a new base upon which to maintain his economic and social standing within his community, but his personality was also a significant influence. Noah had always approached any goal he had set for himself with an unusual degree of single-mindedness. Having decided early in his life to do what was necessary to achieve wealth and status, he did just that. He engaged in trade, lent money to others at a rate that ensured great profitability, and then used the proceeds from these endeavors to acquire slaves and wives, who could help him generate even more profits. But the early to mid-nineteenth century was a difficult time for everyone in Ho, including Yawo. War, drought, a smallpox epidemic, and an earthquake wrought widespread devastation. For Yawo, the final blow came with the death of his beloved older brother. Despite all his efforts, no amount of money, none of his appeals to the gods had helped. Suffering from a serious crisis of faith, Yawo converted to Christianity. He embraced his new religion with the same single-mindedness that had characterized his earlier life. When he was told to retain only one of his three wives, he divorced the other two. When advised to give up his slaves, he did this as well. Yawo's decision to emancipate his slaves came not because of the demands of a colonial law. No European power had yet extended its authority to the Ho area when Yawo released his slaves. Rather, he was motivated by the fact that he could rely on his fellow Christians to assist him economically when necessary, but also because his embrace of his new faith was total.

In presenting the lives of Amegashie, Tamakloe, and Yawo, in revealing both their public and more private concerns, these portraits tell us a great deal about why three slaveholders (and perhaps others) in West Africa responded to abolition as they did. Yet questions remain. Information is often lacking about the influence of others on their decisions. We know, for example, that one of Tamakloe's closest business associates was Paul Sands, that Sands was of slave descent, and that he had written of the anguish he felt when publicly ridiculed because of his social origins. We also know that one of Tamakloe's wives with whom he was particularly close may also have been of slave descent. I have argued here that it was because of these associations, and Tamakloe's own personality, that he came to understand the pain that the institution of slavery inflicted on the enslaved and their descendants. But what of the other slave owners discussed here: Amegashie and Noah Yawo? What was the nature of their associations with their slaves? Were they affected by those associations? Of Amegashie, we only know that he was quite willing to use violence to maintain obedience and that some of his slaves opted to remain with him after the abolition of slavery while others chose to leave. Did he know of their feelings? Did he care? Did their choices to remain or to sever their relations with him influence how Amegashie, himself, responded to abolition? Noah Yawo, like Tamakloe, was married to an enslaved woman. He must certainly have known of his wife's feelings about having been so violently separated from her family, for the European missionaries who knew her documented this. Did Yawo's knowledge of his wife's feelings influence his decision to emancipate his slaves once he converted to Christainity? In missionary accounts, Lydia is portrayed as having strong opinions, even if she chose to express them in a non-confrontational way. Through her behavior and words, did she help give Noah pause about the institution of slavery in ways that eventually led him to take more seriously than perhaps he would have otherwise, the antislavery views of his missionary teachers? What of the influence of other slave owners within their communities? Amegashie, Tamakloe and Yawo were not the only ones forced to respond to abolition. All slave owners faced the same situation. Did peer pressure influence their decisions?[2] And what of the role of those Africans who were associated with the NDMG as teachers, former students, lay liturgists, catechists, and ministers, many of whom were former slaves?. They certainly influenced Yawo in his decision to free his slaves. Was this also true for Tamakloe? Was he moved not only by his close associations with his slave wives and Paul Sands, but also by the antislavery ideas preached by the NDMG missionaries in Anlo? Tamakloe showed little interest in Christianity until the very end of his life. Yet he must have been continually exposed to the notion that slavery was more than simply unfortunate. According to some of his missionary-educated African associates, it was cruel and profoundly unethical. Did his exposure to these new ideas influence how he responded to abolition?

Questions remain as well with regard to the issue of legacies. After each biographical portrait presented in this study, I appended a section that discussed how the decisions made by Amegashie, Tamakloe, and Yawo have continued up to the present to inform relations between their descendants and those of the formerly enslaved. In the case of Amegashie, I argue that his insistence on retaining his slaves as long as possible and his focus on making a sharp distinction between himself, his own immediate family, and those of his slaves generated a legacy in which at least one of his descendants has continued to make such distinctions. Others in West Africa made the same decision; and their decisions, too, have continued to influence family and more general societal relations. Tamakloe's decision to undermine the social hierarchies that distinguished the descendants of the enslaved from others was not universally embraced initially by his own descendants, but in time his approach prevailed. Other families in Ghana and in West Africa, too, followed in his footsteps. As a result, in many places, slave origins has been rendered largely irrelevant in terms of social, political, and economic opportunities. Noah Yawo freed his slaves because he believed that his faith demanded it. He too was not alone in making this kind of decision. Others in West Africa, especially some Muslims, did the same. That faith has continued to play a role in shaping ethical understandings is clear from the actions of local Christian organizations in Ghana, which have been challenging those forms of slavery, old and new, that have been discovered in recent years. In 1997 Mark Wisdom, a Baptist minister, acted on a vision in which he was called by God to free the many *trokosis* (women who were forcibly attached to religious shrines) in southeastern Ghana. His goal: "to take the gospel to the shrines, save *trokosi* priests and functionaries, liberate *trokosi* children and women for Christ, and ultimately cause the prohibition of [the] *trokosi* practice." Although his initial efforts had only limited success, they eventually convinced others in the media to shine a spotlight on the practice in ways that eventually led to the liberation and education of many of the young women attached to the shrines.[3] In the first decade of the twenty-first century, the discovery of children enslaved in Ghana's Lake Volta fishing industry also drew national and international attention. The Ghana government immediately began to address the problem with the cooperation of human rights non-governmental organizations, but it was the Christian social welfare organization, Village of Hope, that came forward to receive rescued children and to provide them with housing, clothing, and educational opportunities.[4] Although it is impossible to draw a direct connection between Noah Yawo's 1877 decision to free his slaves according to his Christian faith and the efforts by modern Christians in Ghana to eradicate slavery in more recent times, Noah's efforts clearly established a path that others have chosen to follow. Local movements have also arisen in other parts of West Africa, especially in Muslim majority countries. There, opponents of the traditional hierarchies that continue to disadvantage those of slave descent have reinterpreted certain religious practices to counter both old and new forms of slavery. In the upper Gambia River basin, for example, the descendants of former slaves have introduced a form of "Islamic reformism . . . [to challenge] the hierarchies of knowledge and learning which have historically [been used to] discriminate against the lower classes."[5] Yet, much more systematic study of these legacies is needed. The lingering stigma of slave origins is known to exist in many areas in West Africa, but how local, how widespread is this phenomenon? I have suggested here that in Ghana the stigma is widely accepted but it is of little significance for most individuals and families in terms of their social, political, economic, or political opportunities. The only known exceptions are those families who hold the most important chieftaincies. But is this really true? Is there a different reality, yet to be discovered and analyzed in Ghana and elsewhere? Are there areas in which slave origins are of greater or lesser significance? If so, what accounts for the differences in legacies within and between different areas? Only with additional research can these questions be addressed.

Notes

Introduction

1. Studies of African responses to conquest and colonial rule constitute a large body of literature that have seen significant shifts over time in how these responses (often termed resistance and accommodation) have been analyzed. For an overview of these shifts, see Cooper, "Conflict and Connection," and Crais, "Resistance and Accommodation."

2. See Greene, "Minority Voices."

3. For a review of post-abolition responses by the enslaved, see Greene, "Minority Voices." Efforts by the enslaved to ameliorate their disadvantaged positions in their communities continued well into the colonial period. See, for example, Berndt, "Closer," and C. A. Brown, "Testing the Boundaries." Studies that focus on efforts by the enslaved and those of slave descent to address ongoing conditions in the postcolonial period are cited in note 9.

4. On slave owners' use of petitions and letters to object to the abolition of slavery and threats to relocate to areas outside colonial jurisdiction, see Klein, *Slavery and Colonial Rule*, 25; Haenger, *Slaves and Slave Holders*, 115; Runkel, "Perspectives"; Getz, "Case for Africans"; Akurang-Parry, "'We Shall Rejoice'"; Akurang-Parry, "'Smattering of Education'"; and for a similar situation in East Africa, Cassanelli, "Ending." On slave owners' use of violence or threats of violence, see Berndt, "Closer," 266–67, 286–87; Klein, *Slavery and Colonial Rule*, 164, 174; Haenger, *Slaves and Slave Holders*, 127, 143; Hall, *A History*, 224–27; and Greene, *Sacred Sites*, 87–88. On slave owners use of colonial courts, see Roberts, *Litigants*, 99–123. On slave owners' redefinition of former slaves as subordinate kin, and on their renegotiation of labor and land relations, see Roberts, "End," 295–96; Haenger, *Slaves and Slave Holders*, 125 and 126; Gaibazzi, "Moving Out," 6–7; and Berndt, "Closer," 267, 283. On slave owners' release of former slaves to manage their own family affairs, see Greene, *West African Narratives*, 142. On the social and cultural politics associated with burials, see Opata, "Remembering Slavery," 61–62; Saha, "Tabula and Pa Jacob," 125; and Brivio, "Evoking the Past," 151, 158. On slave owners' emancipation of slaves prior to the imposition of colonial laws banning such ownership, see Hogendorn and Lovejoy, "Reform"; and Cassanelli, "Ending," 312, 317. For examples of slave owners providing other opportunities so that the formerly enslaved gained greater social and economic independence, see Schmitz, "Islamic Patronage."

5. Miers and Roberts, *End of Slavery*, 33–37.

6. Wright, *Strategies*, 21–43; Greene, *West African Narratives*, 77–102.

7. On the use of the kinship idiom to absorb (or to maintain distinctions) between slaves and their owners when slavery was legal and after, see Lovejoy, *The Ideology* and Mann, *Slavery and the Birth*, 220–30.

8. This spirit of imaginative entrepreneurial innovation is discussed by Pier M. Larson, but in terms of the period of legal slavery in Africa. See his article, "Slaving in Africa."

9. Numerous studies exist on the legacy of slavery in contemporary, postcolonial Africa. See Bellagamba, Greene, and Klein, *Bitter Legacy*. See also Botte, *L'ombre*, and Botte, *Esclavage moderne*. See as well Berndt, "Closer"; de Bruijn and Pelckmans, "Facing Dilemmas"; Hardung, "Curse and Blessing"; Hall, *The History*, 237–40; and Lecocq, "Bellah Question."

10. Biographies of prominent nineteenth-century West African individuals who were slave owners or slave traders that mention, if only cursorily, this aspect of their lives include Hiskett, *Sword of Truth*; Achebe, *Female King*; Falola, "Efusetan Aniwura"; Willis, *In the Path*; Person, *Samori*; Cookey, *King Jaja*; and the biographical sketch of Reverend Henry Charles Bartels in Doortmont, *Pen-Pictures*, 123–25.

11. Such silences are hardly unique to the polity of Anlo. Many others have commented on the same around the history of indigenous slavery in Africa. See, for example, Greene, "Whispers"; Holsey, *Routes*, 61; and Bellagamba, "Reasons."

12. Greene, "Whispers," 48.

13. Thioub, "Regard Critique," 276–77, 279; translation by Eric Brandon, Duke University. For a discussion of the impact of nationalist politics during the colonial period and early independence period on discussions about slavery and the slave trade in Ghana, see Holsey, "Writing" and "Owning Up," 77–78. See also Peterson, "History," 267.

14. See note 6.

15. On the ethical standards established by the American Anthropological Association, see "Principles of Professional Responsibility"; and by the American Historical Association, see *Statement of Standards*. On the ethics and responsibilities of historians who do oral interviewing and on historians' interaction with institutional review boards, see Shopes, "Oral History."

16. Darnton, "Looking."

17. Backscheider, *Reflections*, xv.

18. Nadel, *Biography*, 6.

19. The literature on this very question for Africa is virtually nonexistent. For an overview of the extensive literature on the roots of British abolitionism, see C. L. Brown, *Moral Capital*.

1. Amegashie Afeku of Keta

1. E-mail correspondence with William Sohne, great-grandson of Amegashie Afeku, 1 December 2011.

2. Sohne reports that family memories also depict him as a loving person.

3. Two particularly well-known Western European–trained West African antislavery activitists were David Asante and James "Holy" Johnson. For more on David Asante, see Abun-Nasr, *Afrikaner und Missionar* and "David Asante." See also Addo-Fening, *Akyem-Abuakwa*, 56–68, and Gray, "Legal History," 97–103. On James "Holy" Johnson, see Ayandele, *Holy Johnson*. For an analysis that examines these individuals together with a specific focus on their antislavery activities, see Greene, "Minority Voices."

4. For a recent overview of the reactions of slave owners and the enslaved to abolition in Africa, see Miers, "Slavery to Freedom."

5. He was also a staunch opponent of British colonial rule, not only because of its abolition of slavery, but because he, like many of his fellow Anlo leaders, could not and would not countenance the idea of being controlled by an alien power intent on imposing its own cultural values and supporting its own economic interests above those of the Anlo. Prominent among the Anlo political leaders who fought relentlessly against the British were Tenge and Tsigui from the village of Anyako. Agbodeka, *African Politics*, 62–76; Yegbe, *Anlo*, 120–28.

6. See Strickrodt, *Afro-European*, 75–85.

7. For an early twentieth-century local understanding of the origins of the conflict, see ADM 11/1/1661: Notes of Enquiry, 1912—Awuna, Adda, and Akwamu, 33–34. For Danish accounts of this incident, see Nørregård, *Danish Settlements*, 214–15. For a much more detailed

German missionary account based on Anlo oral traditions collected in the early to mid-nineteenth century, see Hornberger, "Etwas aus der Geschichte der Anloer," 464–66. For a general history of Keta, see Akyeampong, *Between the Sea*.

8. Debrunner, *Church*, 76.

9. Bühler, "Volta Region," 51. Some of these "mulattoes" may have included maternal relatives of Amegashie Afeku, since his mother first had children (who would have been defined as mulattoes at that time) by a Danish-African officer stationed at the fort in Keta during the late eighteenth century before she gave birth to Amegashie Afeku. The Anlo practice patrilineal descent, but they gave considerable weight to matrilineal links during this period. See Greene, *Gender*, chap. 1.

10. Debrunner, *Church*, 76.

11. Unfortunately, population figures are not available for Keta during this period. Instead, there are only general missionary observations about the increasing number of residents.

12. These familial remains must have been those of his maternal rather than paternal relations since we know his father, and later he himself, was buried in the town of Atiavi.

13. *Ocloo v. Amegarshie and others*. In the Supreme Court of the Gold Coast Colony held at Victoriaborg [*sic*], 17 August 1903, before his Honour, Sir W. Brandford Griffith, Chief Justice, 18–20. Court record in the possession of Togbi Amegashie IV, Accra-Nima.

14. The Germans found it difficult to have their claims taken seriously in the local Anlo courts, because they neither respected the Anlo court system, which was overseen, in part, by the very religious authorities whose religion they refused to acknowledge as having any legitimacy, nor were they prepared to have the locals exercise authority over themselves. They were also aware that prior to the 1860s they were viewed with great mistrust by many Anlos.

15. On the history of the Keta Lagoon during this period, see Greene, *Sacred Sites*, chap. 2.

16. Plessing's unwillingness to recognize this law was probably based on his refusal to countenance observation of a legal edict that was based on the very polytheistic religious system that he was dedicated to undermining.

17. The term "fetish priest" was used by Europeans to describe the religious leaders of the polytheistic orders found in Africa. The word fetish comes from the Portuguese word *fetissio*. It was adopted by other Europeans to describe African polytheistic religions, which they erroneously believed involved the worship of material objects rather than the spirits that were believed to occupy those objects.

18. "Ein Alter Heide," 80–84; Müller, *Geschichte*, 41.

19. In 1865, when Anlo came into conflict with the British, this time on the battlefield, and they lost more than a hundred men without capturing a single enemy, it was a group of businessmen/elders—no doubt a group that included Amegashie Afeku—who persuaded the despondent warriors not to seek revenge for their losses on the missionaries in their midst. As noted by the missionaries at the time: "the elders rejected the proposal of their young warriors by asking: 'when you have palm oil, to whom do you bring it? And if you need something, where do you go to buy it?'" At this point the missionaries were no longer seen as just another form of British presence. Instead, they were recognized as Germans, as missionaries who kept their distance from political matters in order to focus on religious affairs, and who had become important business partners. See "Giraldo und der Kampf der Angloer gegen die Adaer," document in the author's possession. Accordingly, when the German missionaries expanded into the interior towns to further propagate their faith, they did so with the support of those businessmen in Keta, among them Amegashie, who had linked their own success in trade to the success of the missionary expansionary efforts. This was most evident in the late 1860s when the missionaries posted to the interior village of Waya found themselves threatened with

death by an invading Asante army and subject to highway robbery when they fled to the coast. It was Amegashie who sent men to rescue them. See Merz, "Waya" (20, no. 240 [1870]; "Der Krieg," [1870] 1039–40.

20. See Akyeampong, *Between the Sea*, 82–84.

21. Greene, *Gender*, 102–5.

22. Greene, Field Note 69: Interview with Dzobi Adzinku, 7 January 1988, Anloga; Field Note 70: Interview with Kwami Kpodo, 12 January 1988, Woe; Field Note 77: Interview with Kwami Kpodo, 20 January 1988, Woe.

23. Other family sources indicate that he had twelve wives. See Greene, Field Note 92: Interview with Amegashie IV, 19 February 1998, Accra-Nima. Sohne, *Genealogical Trees*, 6–7.

24. Sohne, *Genealogical Trees*, 6. These merchants included the Williams, the Adjorlolos, the Van Lares, and the Tamakloes.

25. "Ein Aergerlicher Auftritt."

26. Schiek, "Keta," 1193. Anlos called the staff *zofue*. Its symbolic and religious significance is unclear although the cord was probably the type of necklace that only priests wore. See Greene, Field Note 96: Interview with Anthonio Gbordzor II and his councilors, 24 February 1988, Woe.

27. For more on missionary approaches to the clothing and their fascination with the rich textiles often favored by Africans, see Hay, "Changes," and Byfield, "Dress." See also Geary, "Missionary."

28. The missionaries suffered the same treatment, but were finally able to extricate themselves from the ban by convincing the Anlo leadership that they were neither British nor Danes, but Germans who were there not to threaten them, but to convert them to Christianity. The fact that the missionaries lent the paramount chief money that he could use to pay the debts of his son, and the fact that they also expressed an interest in trade (rather than gunboat diplomacy) also helped their case. Bremen Staatsarchiv: Norddeutschen Missions-Gesellschaft, 7, 1025: Letter from B. Schlegel, Keta, to Norddeutschen Missionsgesellschaft, Bremen, 23 January 1857.

29. Hostility was especially strong among the residents of Anyako and other nearby towns. This set of villages, especially Anyako—located on the north side of the Keta Lagoon—had become the principle center where individuals from the interior brought their goods to exchange them for commodities originating either from Europe or from the towns and villages on the Atlantic littoral. Under the leadership of Anyako chiefs Tsigui and Tenge, the interior Anlo population was hostile not only to the British but also to the Bremen missionaries, as the latter sought to expand their evangelical and trading activities into the interior. As mentioned, Amegashie was not hostile toward the Bremen Mission at all after some time, but he did share with Tsigui and Tenge a deep hatred of British colonial rule. On Tenge and Tsigui's resistance to British colonial policies, see Agbodeka, *African Politics*, 62–76. On Tenge and Tsigui's efforts to maintain their trade interests (which put them in opposition not only to the British but also to many of the chiefs on the Anlo littoral), see also Yegbe, *Anlo*, 120–29.

30. ADM 41/4/1–2: Criminal and Civil Record Book, 27 May 1884 to 16 November 1888 and 9 June 1884 to 14 January 1888—*Genardoo v. Moshi*, 27 September 1888, District Commissioner's Court, Quittah; ADM 41/1/25: Minute Books—A.M.K. to the Honorable, the Colonial Secretary, 28 December 1891, and A.M.K., District Commissioner, to the District Commissioner, Kwitta, 29 January 1892.

31. On the reasons for Nyigbla's loss of popularity, see Greene, *Gender*, 81–102 and 112–17.

32. Knowing how sensitive this subject continues to be in Ghana and the fact that the publication of this biography might have unintended consequences for the descendants of

Amegashie Afeku, I consulted with the family. After reading the penultimate draft, William Sohne—an Amegashie Afeku descendant and the Amegashie family historian—agreed to support the publication because, it "is a purely academic undertaking [and] not a sensation-seeking journalistic exposé." In addition, he noted that, "being a foreigner," I had "no axe to grind with the Amegashies." He argued as well that the status of Amegashie's maternal grand-mother—discussed later in this chapter—was and is not a big issue in the patrilineal Anlo system." E-mail correspondence, 29 November and 1 December 2011. Readers should note that Sohne's remark about the status of Amegashie's maternal grandmother reflects recent trends in Anlo reckonings of kinship relations. Since the mid-twentieth century, the Anlo have in-creasingly shifted from a system in which women as sisters were recognized as essential to a system of inheritance in which their sons could inherit acquired property from these women's brothers (their maternal uncles) to a more purely patrilineal system. This, in turn, has influ-enced the emphasis on remembering the status of the women in any given family. Women rarely inherit land now and their sons rarely inherit anything from their maternal uncles. Accordingly, the status of women in Anlo has increasingly become marginal in Anlo family histories. On the importance of women in Anlo family histories prior to the mid-twentieth century and on the shift in their status since that time, see Greene, *Gender.*

33. SC 14/1–14: The Old Diary—Remarkable Occurrences of the Gold Coast and Ashanti.

34. Greene, Field Note 91: Interview with Amegashie Afeku, 18 February 1988, Accra-Nima. Such relationships between European men and enslaved African women were not uncommon and have been examined by George E. Brooks in a number of his publications, including *Landlords*, 137; "Signares"; and "Nhara." See also Greene, "Crossing Boundaries," and for an excellent study of and update on the most recent literature on this topic, Ipsen, *Daughters.*

35. Merz, *Ein Neger-Gehuelte*, 14.

36. Schiek, "Keta," 1193–94. While the Nyigbla religious order's reputation in Anlo had been damaged, in the 1830s, in part because of its involvement in the sale of its own members into the slave trade, it still wielded influence in the Anlo capital.

37. Merz, "Ein trauriges Reiseerlebniss," 73–75.

38. To date I have been unable to locate the actual court case. Instead, this description relies on the background information on Amegashie that colonial officials penned for their superiors when Amegashie was prosecuted for slave trading in the 1880s. This background information can be found in the following records: ADM 11/1/1107: W.B.G., Accra, to the Right Honorable F. A. Stanley, M.P., Gold Coast Colony, 22 July 1885; ADM 12/3/1 (Confidential Gold Coast Dispatches from the Governor to the Secretary of State, 4 March 1881–21 March 1887): Qaiule Jones, New Site, to the Right Honorable Earl Granville, K.G., 15/4/85), 383–85. The only thing the government could do was confiscate his property (including his land) at Keta.

39. SC 14/1: Old Diary, 211.

40. ADM 1/2/23: H. T. Ussher, Quittah Fort to the Right Honorable Sir Michael Hicks, M.P., 6 December 1879.

41. On Bannerman's views on slavery and his support for this institution, which may ex-plain why he was more than willing to defend Amegashie against accusations of slave dealing, see Runkel, "An African Abolitionist."

42. "Ein Alter Heide," 80–84.

43. ADM 41/4/21: *Quashie Moshi of Quittah v. Amegashie of Afiengbah,* 25 January 1886, 137–45.

44. ADM 41/1/21: *Regina v. Amegashie District Commissioner's Court,* Kwitta, 17 December 1889, 393.

45. Amegashie insisted on defying the British antislavery ordinances even as he was deeply protective of the German missionaries, a group that was just as committed as the British to altering the very foundations upon which Anlo society rested. Yes, it is true that the Bremen Mission, in particular, did not take an open stance against slavery, but its religious mission did seek to challenge the Nyigbla order with which Amegashie was affiliated. We can only assume that he was not threatened by this, and that his ability to benefit from their business activities far outweighed their often unsuccessful efforts to convert the Anlo to Christianity.

46. Schlegel, "Beitrag zur Geschichte," 398.

47. Haenger, *Slaves and Slave Holders*, 127. Another case of the use of violence against slaves escaping to the coast is cited in this case study on p. 143.

48. See Greene, *Sacred Sites*, 87–88.

49. Berndt, "Closer," 266–67.

50. Klein, *Slavery and Colonial Rule*, 164.

51. Berndt, "Closer," 286–87.

52. King Jaja of the Niger is arguably the most well-known individual of slave descent who became a prominent political and economic leader in the region where he lived. Numerous biographies of him exist. Some of the earlier studies include Dike, *Trade*; Jones, *Trading States*; and Horton, "From Fishing Village." For a somewhat more recent study, see Cookey, *King Jaja*. See also Sean Stilwell, *Paradoxes of Power*, whose book is not biographical; instead, he discusses royal slaves in more general terms. Still he provides enough examples to show that even the status of these individuals did not mitigate their slave status. See, in particular, 154–56.

53. How did black slave owners, most of whom were also of slave descent, respond to abolition in the United States? Studies on this group do not directly address this question. Instead, they focus on what these owners did not do. As noted by Larry Koger, "most black owners did not intend to manumit their slaves and viewed the institution of slavery as a source of labor to be exploited for their own benefit. . . . [Their] attitudes and actions . . . appear to be similar to those of the white slave owners." Koger, *Black Slave owners*, 2–3. See also Johnson and Roark, *Black Masters*, 133.

54. I do not include a reference here to maintain the confidentiality of this interviewee.

55. A similar situation developed in Senegal in 2007. See Thioub, "Stigmas," 9.

56. See Bellagamba, Greene, and Klein, *Bitter Legacy*, 13. Note that the specific law in question in Ghana, the 1874 ordinances banning slavery, made provisions for "local custom" to limit the new laws in some cases. The ordinance states explicitly that "nothing herein contained shall be construed to diminish or derogate from the rights and obligations of parents and of children, or for other rights and obligations, not being repugnant to the laws of England, arising out of the family and tribal relations customarily used and observed in the Protected Territories." I thank Trevor Getz for this more precise reading of the ordinances.

57. Duffy, "*Hadijatou Mani Koroua v Niger.*" The decision made by the Niger court was eventually overturned by the Community Court of Justice of the Economic Community of West African States in 2008.

58. On the ways in which colonial and post-colonial developments have altered the economic hierarchies that characterized the slavery period in some ways but maintained them in others, see Bellagamba, "The Legacies."

59. Lecocq, "Bellah Question," 55–56.

60. Lecocq, "Bellah Question," 58. See also Thioub, "Stigmas," 8, 9.

61. See, for example, Hardung, "Curse and Blessing"; de Bruijn and Pelckmans, "Facing Dilemmas"; McDougall, "Living," as well as other articles in *Esclavage moderne ou modernité de l'esclavage?*, ed. Roger Botte, special issue *Cahiers d'Études Africaines* 179–80 (2005); Salem, "Bare-Foot Activists"; and Hahonou, "Past and Present."

2. Nyaho Tamakloe of Anlo

1. Katechist Elias Tamakloe, "Notzen über den alten Tamakloe," Bremen Staatsarchiv: Norddeutschen Missions-Gesellschaft, 7, 1025, Keta: 14/1. See also C. Spiess, "Bedeutung," which contains a list of drinking names with their meanings.

2. Tamakloe died in 1918.

3. On the use of euphemisms, see the citations in note 30. On the continued stigma of slave origins, see Bellagamba, Greene, and Klein, *Bitter Legacy*.

4. On the history of Euro-Africans in Anlo after 1807, see Greene, *Gender*, 93–95, 127–34.

5. See the document attached to Greene, Field Note 74: Kuetuade-Tamaklo, The Life and Times, 3.

6. While these wars were largely local, the different sides frequently approached others who had common political concerns to provide them with additional troops. In the 1769 war, Ada was offered or received support from Akyem, Anecho, and the "so-called" River Negroes in Mafi and Agave. In the 1784 Sabadre war, it received support from the same polities that had aided it in 1769 with the addition of forces from Accra and Akuapem.

7. On the Atiteti war (also known as the Funu war), see A. B. Horton, *Letters*, 75–89. On the Agoue war, see Gaba, "History of Anecho," 127–39; and Strickrodt, *Afro-European*, 184–94. See also Bouché, *La Côte des ésclaves*, 303. On the Glover or Gbedzidzavu war, see Yegbe, Anlo, 88–92.

8. On Anlo fears of an Asante invasion of their home territory, see J. Illg and J. Müller, "Der Afrikanische Krieg," 1071.

9. ADM 11/1/1661: Notes of Evidence, Commission of Enquiry, 1912, Awuna, Adda, and Akwamu, 82–83. Tamakloe, himself, was also wounded in the hip.

10. ADM 11/1/1661: Notes of Evidence, Commission of Enquiry, 1912, Awuna, Adda, and Akwamu, 33–34.

11. On Axolu's refusal to return to Anloga, the capital of the Anlo polity, because of defeats he had suffered, see Anlo State Council Minute Book, 9 January 1935: Testimony of Davordji Baninin in the court case of *Chiefs Kata, Adaku Avege, and Agbevo . . . on behalf of the Tsiame Tribe of Anloga, etc v. Chiefs Zewu, Agbozo, etc on behalf of the Agave Tribe of Anloga, etc*, 378. See also Yegbe, Anlo, 79–80 who offers another explanation for Axolu's actions. Yegbe claims Axolu felt humiliated when many Anlos refused to accompany him to the Agoue war.

12. Anlo State Council Minute Book, 9 January 1935: Testimony of Davordji Baninin in the court case of *Chiefs Kata, Adaku Avege, and Agbevo . . . on behalf of the Tsiame Tribe of Anloga, etc v. Chiefs Zewu, Agbozo, etc on behalf of the Agave Tribe of Anloga, etc*, 379–84.

13. Anlo State Council Minute Book, 9 January 1935: Testimony of Davordji Baninin in the court case of *Chiefs Kata, Adaku Avege, and Agbevo . . . on behalf of the Tsiame Tribe of Anloga, etc v. Chiefs Zewu, Agbozo, etc on behalf of the Agave Tribe of Anloga, etc*, p. 383.

14. Greene, Field Note 74: Interview with A. W. Kuetuade-Tamaklo, 19 January 1988, Tegbi.

15. Greene, Field Note 74: Interview with A. W. Kuetuade-Tamaklo, 19 January 1988, Tegbi.

16. These various financial transactions have been culled from the following sources: SC 12/1: G. B. Williams Papers; Yegbe, Anlo, 119, 121; ADM 41/1/3: W. A. Caseaden, District Commissioner, Quittah, 20 June 1882; ADM 11/1/1185: Awuna Native Affairs—Joachim Acolatse, Chief, Quittah, 16 February 1920, to The Honorable, the Secretary for Native Affairs, Accra; Greene, *West African Narratives*, 172, 175, 177; ADM 11/1/1113: J. M. Agbosome to the Governor, 5 March 1884; Judicial Council Minute Book, 1913: *Heyman v. Chief Tamakloe*, Quittah, 22 July 1813, p. 121; Documents held by Christian Tamakloe, Keta, accessed January 1988: (a) Indenture, 11 October 1904, (b) Agreement, between Avonokete and Avagashie of Jellacoffi on the

one part and Chief Nyaho Tamakloe of Quittah on the other part, (c) Agreement between King Amegbor and Chiefs and Headmen of Klikor and Chief Nyaho Tamakloe of Hutey, (d) Indenture between George Briggance Wiliams of Freetown, Sierra Leone . . . and Chief Nyaho Tamaklo of Kwittah, 1902, (e) Memorandum of Agreement between Thomas Wulff Cochrane of Acra and Chief Nyaho Tamakloe of Kwittah (and accompanying documents), (f) Copy of Supreme Court case *M. A. Williams v. Chief Tamakloe*, 17 December 1906, (g) Agreement between Chief N. Tamakloe of Keta and Messrs. Bodecker and Meyer, 31 May 1907, (h) Copy of Judgment: Tetu Creek and Hillock, 7 November 1908, (i) Native court of Fia Sri II, Anloga: *Chief Tamakloe of Keta v. Klu Tsiamehia Lumo, Anyigblako Gbogbokuku of Dekpo*, 18 April 1910; SC 12/6: G. B. Williams Papers—Order for goods, Chief Tamaklo of Hootie, 1887.

17. Tamakloe is remembered as having ties to the Williams family through Francis Awoonor Williams, his sister's son, also known as Kwame Borbor Tamakloe, who he sent to England for education as a lawyer. Greene, Field Note 74: Interview with A. W. Kuetuade-Tamaklo, 19 January 1988, Tegbi. In addition to Francis Awoonor Williams, Tamakloe sent his son, Benjamin, for legal education in Britain. Julius Michael Hia, who worked for a time as a commission clerk at the Bremen Mission factory also helped him establish legal claim to his property. See documents held by Christian Tamakloe, Keta, accessed January 1988: Native court of Fia Sri II, Anloga: *Chief Tamakloe of Keta v. Klu Tsiamehia Lumo, Anyigblako Gbogbokuku of Dekpo*, 18 April 1910; Greene, Field Note 74: Interview with A. W. Kuetuade-Tamaklo, 19 January 1988, Tegbi.

18. Greene, *West African Narratives*, 170–71. These sons were Edward, John, Samuel, and Henry.

19. On English language instruction by the Catholics, see Debrunner, *Church*, 113.

20. According to the Tamakloe family history, he had 150 children. Greene, Field Note 74: Interview with A. W. Kuetuade-Tamaklo, 19 January 1988, Tegbi.

21. Greene, Field Note 97: Interview with J. W. Kodzo-Vordoagu, 24 February 1988.

22. Greene, Field Note 97: Interview with J. W. Kodzo-Vordoagu, 24 February 1988.

23. C. Spiess, "Fünfzig Jahre," 4.

24. Cited in Greene, *West African Narratives*, 144.

25. Cited in Greene, *West African Narratives*, 144.

26. All these proverbs were collected by German missionary Bernhard Schlegel and Anlo seminary students and teachers (including J. Quist and R. Kwami) between 1857 and 1915. See Bürgi, "Sammlung von Ewe-Sprichwötern," 417, 425, 427, 432, 433, and 435.

27. *Parliamentary Papers, 1975*, 27; emphasis mine.

28. Ustorf, *Bremen Missionaries*, 310–11.

29. Gold Coast, 1898.

30. Greene, Field Note 63: Interview with L. A. Banini, 5 January 1988, Anloga. Similar practices developed elsewhere. On the situation in Ho, see Spieth, *Ewe*, 182.

31. Greene, Field Note 57: Interview with Robert G. Kofi Afetogbo, 22 December 1987, Anloga. On the practice of Afa (known as Ifa among the Yoruba), see Surgy, *La géomancie*.

32. Greene. Field Note 72: Interview with Christian Nani Tamakloe, 13 January 1988, Keta.

33. ADM 1/2/ 23: H. T. Ussher, Governor, Quittah, to the Right Honorable Sir Michael Hicks-Beach, Bart, M.P., 23 November 1879.

34. Greater Anlo refers to those polities, for example Weta, Avenor and Klikor, that regularly aligned with Anlo during conflicts with other polities beginning in the second half of the eighteenth century. See Greene, "The Anlo-Ewe," 152.

35. Central Anlo, also known as Anlo Akuaku, consists of towns that were incorporated into the Anlo polity by 1741. See Greene, "The Anlo-Ewe," 151.

36. The chief who caught the attention of the British for engaging in this business was Aco-latse of Kedzi, Tamakloe's friend and comrade-in-arms in the Agoue war. See ADM 11/1/113, Part 2: Francis A. Lamb, District Commissioner, Kwitta, to the Honorable, the Colonial Secretary, Victoriaborg, 24 September 1889. That Tamakloe was involved in this same scheme is suggested by the very close ties that existed between him and Acolaste. Not only did they fight together in the Agoue war, Acolatse was Tamakloe's uncle. They also conducted a great deal of business together. When Acolatse established a store at Bey Beach, Tamakloe followed several years later. Both owned land in Keta for which immigrant Hausa settlers paid rent. Both evicted these settlers at the same time in July of 1909 when they were unable to afford the rent of one shilling per month per house. The total number of houses was between four hundred and five hundred. See the GPRAA Regional Office at Ho: Item No. 14, Case No. 5.82: Haussa Community—John Maxwell, Commissioner of the Eastern Province, Quittah, to the Honorable Colonial Secretary, Accra, 8 October 1909. The collaboration between the Klikor chief and Tamakloe for this purpose is also verified in Greene, Field Note 74: Interview with A. W. Kuetuade-Tamaklo, 19 January 1988, Tegbi.

37. On the history of trade to Anecho, see Bühler, "Volta Region," 113–24.

38. ADM 11/1/1661: Testimony of Nyaho Tamakloe before the Commission of Enquiry, 1912, Awuna, Adda, and Akwamu, p. 97.

39. ADM 11/1/1661: Testimony of Nyaho Tamakloe before the Commission of Enquiry, 1912, Awuna, Adda, and Akwamu, p. 92.

40. Katechist Elias Tamakloe, "Notzen über den alten Tamakloe," Bremen Staatsarchiv: Norddeutschen Missions-Gesellschaft, 7, 1025, Keta: 14/1.

41. ADM 11/1/1661: Testimony of Nyaho Tamakloe before the Commission of Enquiry, 1912, Awuna, Adda, and Akwamu, 52. See also Katechist Elias Tamakloe, "Notzen über den alten Tamakloe," Bremen Staatsarchiv: Norddeutschen Missions-Gesellschaft, 7, 1025, Keta: 14/1. For a discussion of the selection and enstoolment process by someone who was the linguist for Amedor Kpegla and who served as a functionary at the enstoolment of the Adzovia clan's candidate, see SC 14/3: Customs and Ceremonies performed at the Enstoolment of Awoame Fia (King) of Anlo (Awuna) as related by (Dutsiama) State Linguist Ahovia Fiahogbe, a court official of late Awoame Fia Amedor Kpegla, and one of the functionaries at the Enstoolment of the present Fia Sri II., 302–14. See also Greene, Field Note 74: Interview with A. W. Kuetuade-Tamaklo, 19 January 1988, Tegbi, on the composition of the delegation.

42. See Greene, *West African Narratives*, 151.

43. Greene, Field Note 53: Interview with Afatsao Awadzi, 16 December 1987, Anloga.

44. Greene, *Sacred Sites*, 120; Greene, Field Note 69: Interview with Dzobi Adzinku, 7 January 1988, Anloga. Greene, Field Note 57: Interview with Robert G. Kofi Afetogbo, 22 December 1987, Anloga.

45. Fia Sri II definitely supported modernization, but he like Tamakloe, also believed that much in Anlo culture had value. When the British sought to outlaw a number of different religious groups, he successfully resisted the banning of some of the more established groups, Nyigba and Yewe. See Greene, *Sacred Sites*, 120; Greene, Field Note 69: Interview with Dzobi Adzinku, 7 January 1988, Anloga.

46. Judicial Council Record Book, 1914: Summons Book of Anloga, Suit No. 159/14, in the Native Tribunal of Fia Sri II of Anlo, 20 July 1914. Defamation cases, in which hefty fines were levied against individuals who called other persons slaves, are recorded as early as 1891. The colonial government prosecuted these cases, but they did so in accordance with local law. See ADM 41/1/1–2: Criminal and Civil Record Book, 27 May 1884–16 November 1888, and 9 June 1884 to 14 January 1888: 6 March 1891, Claim: £15 for defamation of character. On local

Anlo laws about revealing the background of those of slave descent, several elders emphasized the severity of the punishment for doing so: "It is against the law to reveal . . . their origins. . . . If you dare say it, your father's property could be transferred to the slave, leaving you with nothing." "It's not allowed to discuss the origins of a person, to know that they are slaves . . . it is a serious case. . . . Prosperity comes to the owner through the slave and so they don't want to refer to their origins. . . . No court will allow [such testimony]. If you don't know and try [to reveal the origins] you are revealing the secrets of all the families in the town." Greene, Field Note 60: Interview with Tete Za Agbemako, 5 January 1987, Anloga; and Greene, Field Note 54: Interview with Tse Gbeku, 16 December 1987, Anloga, respectively.

47. Greene, Field Note 54: Interview with Tse Gbeku, 16 December 1987, Anloga.

48. Greene, Field Note 70: Interview with Kwami Kpodo, Woe, 12 January 1988.

49. Others note that making no such distinctions between the children of slave and free wives was not unusual approach for other slave masters in Anlo. See Greene, Field Note 52: Interview with Dzobi Adzinku, 15 December 1987, Anloga; Field Note 59: Interview with Amawota Amable, 23 December 1987, Anloga.

50. See Greene, *West African Narratives*, 177.

51. Reinke, "Eine Doppelfeier," 83–84.

52. On Anlo songs about loss as well as love composed from the late nineteenth to the mid-to-late twentieth century by noted poets from the polity, see Awoonor, *Guardians*.

53. His uncle and good friend, Joachim Acolatse, did the same but was eventually caught and prosecuted by the British.

54. See the following documents appended to Greene, Field Note 74: The House of Togbui Kpeku Nyaho Tamakloe; and The Last Will, Testament and Codicil of the Late Togbui Nyaho Tamakloe I.

55. Greene, Field Note 74: Interview with A. W. Kuetuade-Tamaklo, 19 January 1988, Tegbi.

56. Schmitz, "Islamic Patronage," 92–93.

57. According to Valsecchi, "My Dearest Child Is My Slave's Child," local informants stated that individuals from a "spurious" line, were installed "due to a lack of suitable candidates" within the "pure" line.

58. Valsecchi, "My Dearest Child."

59. An extensive body of literature exists on how the formerly enslaved responded to abolition and the opportunities they seized to overcome both their social, political, and economic marginalization. For an excellent overview of the literature on this topic and an outstanding analysis of migrations by former slaves, see Rossi, "Migration and Emancipation."

60. On recent political movements to combat the continued legacy of slavery in contemporary West Africa, see Hahonou, "Slavery and Politics"; Salem, "Bare-Foot Activists," 156–77; Botte, "Riimayɓe, Ḥarāṭīn, Iklan"; Hahonou and Pelckmans, "West African Antislavery Movements"; and Jeanne, "La mise en scène."

3. Noah Yawo of Ho-Kpenoe

1. Spieth, *Ewe*, 175. Spieth served as a missionary with the Norddeutschen Missions-Gesellschaft in the Ewe-speaking areas of what is now Ghana and Togo from 1880 to 1911. The author of many publications on the Ewe people and their language, Spieth knew Ho very well, having served there numerous times: 1880 to 1881, 1885 to 1888, 1889 to 1892, 1893 to 1897, and 1898 to 1902. See Schreiber, *Bausteine zur Geschichte*, 216–17, 234–36.

2. In describing Yawo as a slave owner, and in discussing those slaves who were under his authority, I include individuals acquired through purchase as well as debt slaves, the latter of

whom could easily become bought individuals if the debt for which they were to be enslaved was not repaid. The Ewe distinguished these types of individuals, debt and purchased slaves, from war captives, but the information we have about Yawo does not allow us to identify exactly how many slaves he had at any given time, or the origins of their enslavement. His future wife, Lydia, was captured; and he certainly held debt slaves, but he also inherited a number of slaves from his brother, about whom we know little.

3. Debrunner, *Church*, 97; Bremen Staatsarchiv: 7, 1025–12/2: Letter from Joseph Reindorf to Gentlemen, 10 July 1875.

4. "Noch Einmal Ho," 9–12. See also Bremen Staatsarchiv: 7, 1025–12/2: Letter from Joseph Reindorf to Gentlemen, 10 July 1875; Debrunner, *Church*, 97.

5. On Christian converts who refused to give up their slaves and debt pawns, see Mallet, "Briefe," 137–38. See also Haenger, *Slaves and Slave Holders*, 75–111 and 173. Haenger explores the lives of a number of African Christian catechists associated with the Switzerland-based Basel Mission on the Gold Coast, the majority of whom refused to give up their slaves and debt pawns. See also his 1993 interview with Koranteng Ata-Caesar, 182–91, whose great-grandfather did liberate his slaves upon converting to Christianity.

6. German missionaries who knew Yawo estimated he was about forty years of age in 1872. Müller, *Geschichte*, 178.

7. Most of these polities consisted of only five or six villages or towns. For a 1915 account of these polities, see ADM 39/5/7: Ho District Record Book, which contains a report by R. S. Rattray on the towns and villages in the former German Togoland.

8. ADM 39/5/7: Ho District Record Book. Rattray's report contains accounts of resistance to Asante and Akwamu aggression, but also memories of local conflicts over land, slave raiding by neighbors, and other disputes.

9. In 1818 the polity of Wusuta engaged in passive resistance by refusing to contribute troops for Asante's war in Gyaman. Earlier, it had evaded Asante's annual raids by relocating its towns further away from the Volta River. See Rattray, *Ashanti Law*, 261.

10. For a history of Akwamu military actions and Krepi resistance to the same between the 1760s and 1813, based on European documentary sources, see Kea, "Akwamu-Anlo Relations," 33–34. For oral traditions about the conflicts between Akwamu and the local polities in Krepi, see Spieth, *Ewe*, 82–90. For an excellent analysis of these wars, based on both oral traditions and documentary sources, see Asare, "Akwamu-Peki Relations." See, for example, his discussion of the Awudome revolt against Akwamu in 1829, 66–71. Conflicts between Krepi forces and Asante were also recorded in both documentary and oral traditions. See Greene, *West African Narratives*, 101, and contemporary newspaper accounts. A massive revolt in Krepi against Asante occurred, for example, in 1823 that included not only the Krepi polities, but also Asante's past ally, Akwamu, as well Anlo. In his study, "Akwamu-Peki Relations," Asare explains the larger political context in which this revolt occurred. For documentary sources on this conflict, see reports printed in 1823 in a number of issues of the *Royal Gold Coast Gazette and Commercial Intelligencer*, which documented the campaign against the Asantes: 21, 28 January; 18 March; 15 April; 20 May; 14, 21 June; 9, 16, 23, 30 August; 8, 22 November; 13 December.

11. Trade embargoes were a common tactic used against Asante by those who sought to limit its power even before the abolition of the slave trade in 1807. See Fynn, *Asante*, 41–48, 61, 63–66; Yarak, "Political Consolidation," 17–30; Tenkorang, "Importance of Firearms," 5–6.

12. On the trade routes in Krepi and on the Volta River over which there was much competition for control, see Greene, *Gender*, 56–58; Kea, "Akwamu-Anlo Relations," 56–61; Johnson, "Ashanti," 41–44. Akwamu and Asante were not without friends in Krepi. One of the most important was the polity of Peki. On Peki's relations with Akwamu and the reasons they

eventually turned against their Akwamu ally, see Asare, "Akwamu-Peki Relations," 36–40, 62–63, and 71–74; and Sorkpor, "Role," 4–5. On the character of Akwamu rule in Krepi, see Asare, "Akwamu-Peki Relations."

13. These two states had dominated the region since 1733.

14. Bühler, "Volta Region," 92–93.

15. The trade involved the exchange of local coastal produce (salt and preserved fish) as well as European trade goods (cloth, liquor, metal ware, guns, gunpowder) purchased from the Danish, English, and Portuguese traders operating on the coast, for commodities produced in the interior (palm oil, yams, cotton, slaves, ivory). But this trade had never been very large. The subsistence farmers in both areas produced many of the goods they consumed; trade was largely in products that they and their customers could not obtain locally.

16. This policy affected not only traders from the Krepi district, but also those from Asante and Akwamu who brought their slaves for sale to the Anlo village of Atorkor. On this trade, see Greene, *West African Narratives*, 190–91.

17. Weyhe, "Wegbe," 551.

18. Bühler, "Volta Region," 72–73.

19. On the history of Anyako, its rise after the 1847 destruction of Keta by the Danes and its status as major center of trade with the interior and later as a center of east-west smuggling after the extension of British colonial rule, see Sorkpor, Geraldo De Lima.

20. On the various ways in which people during this period acquired wealth, see Spieth, *Ewe*, 175.

21. Akwamu made two attempts between 1845 and 1869 to regain control over Krepi. The first occurred in 1845. The second, remembered only in local oral traditions, is not recorded in any documentary sources, although references are made to a possible conflict erupting in 1852. See Asare, "Akwamu-Peki Relations," 84 and 87.

22. Hornberger, "Wegbe" (12, no. 142 [1862]): 619–20; "Noah Yawo."

23. "Noah Yawo," 332.

24. The school in Ho began initially with four boys from Peki (where in 1847 the NDMG had established its first missionary station), and with several enslaved children whom the missionaries bought and freed. See Hornberger, "Wegbe" (11, no. 125 [1861]): 570. Hesitation on the part of the people of Ho to send their children to the missionary school was based on concerns similar to those held by other Ewe-speaking parents. Their children's attendance could be seen by others as an indication that the family had fallen into debt and had to pawn a child to the missionaries in exchange for some form of assistance from them. While pawning was a common practice, most people found it embarrassing and something to avoid. See C. Spiess, "Fünfzig Jahre," 4. See also Bühler, "Volta Region," 61–62.

25. Spieth, *Ewe*, 31, listed these towns as Kpenoe, Akoviefe, Banyakoe, Heve, and Ahliha.

26. Hornberger, "Wegbe" (12, no. 142 [1862]): 619–20.

27. Hornberger, "Wegbe" (12, no. 142 [1862]): 619–20.

28. Müller, *Geschichte*, 62–64. At least eight women missionaries worked in Ho between 1859 and 1869, six of whom died there. See Schreiber, *Bausteine zur Geschichte*, 241, and R. Illg, "Was Frau Illg von Ho erzählt," 404–10.

29. See Spieth, *Ewe*, 345–60, 403, on yam cultivation in Ho.

30. Spieth, *Ewe*, 345–55.

31. Hornberger, Untitled, 685–89. See also "Ein Fetisch Priester," 49–64, in which Tenu Kwami's life history is retold, but with far fewer details about the financial demands that Tenu Kwami faced when becoming a priest. On local cowrie currencies in this region, in which a string consisted of between forty and fifty cowries, and a head of between two thousand

and two thousand five hundred cowries, see Marion Johnson, "The Cowrie Currencies," both Parts I and II; and Robin Law, "Computing Domestic Prices."

32. Others elsewhere in the Krepi region expressed similar frustrations with local priests. See Meyer, *Translating the Devil*, 97.

33. Hornberger, "Fetischwesen in Wegbe," 731.

34. "Noah Yawo," 332.

35. On Ewe ideas about how to deal with smallpox, see Greene, *West African Narratives*, 65; "Wie man zu Anyako," 321–24.

36. As noted by Christian Hornberger, the local priests in Ewe-speaking areas like Ho were responsible for devising remedies to address spiritual as well as physical health problems. This was not necessarily the case elsewhere in West Africa, however. Hornberger, "Neger-Doctoren," 1313–14. See also, "Ein Fetish Priester," 58–60, in which the author describes, from his own perspective, priestly medical practices in Ho.

37. Zündel, "Afrika," 802–4.

38. Hornberger, "Neger-Doctoren," 1313–14.

39. Rattray, *Ashanti Law*, 261. For a discussion of what little is known about Asante political activity in Krepi, see Wilks, *Asante*, 57, 68, 321, and Kea, "Akwamu-Anlo Relations," 54.

40. For a fuller discussion see Asare, "Akwamu-Peki Relations," 80–84; and Sorkpor, "Role," 8. See also Maier, "Asante War Aims."

41. Merz, "Waya" (21, no. 247 [1871]): 1116; Binder, "Verhandlungen wegen Waya," 1112; "Der Krieg" (20, no. 231 [1870]): 1037; "Der Krieg" (20, no. 229 [1870]): 1030.

42. On the supplying of firearms and gunpowder to Asante by Anlo in the past, see Greene, *Gender*, 121–22, 129.

43. On this shift from the export of slave labor to agricultural produce in Anlo, see Greene, *Gender*, 128. It is important to note that many in Anlo did not agree with the idea of participating in a war in Krepi. These individuals had established trade relations with many communities there and they feared the negative impact on their businesses (even as they faced more competition from the missionary-trained Africans who had begun to use their contacts with the NDMG to purchase goods from the interior and market them directly to the Europeans on the coast). An additional concern for Anlo was their mistrust of Asante. See "Kriegsnachrichten aus Afrika," 995–97.

44. For a description of the Agotime war as described by the NDMG missionaries, see J. Illg and J. Müller, "Der Ashanti Krieg," 1009–11.

45. For a more detailed description of these battles from the perspective of a Ho citizen who participated in them, see Spieth, *Ewe*, 94–104. On the lead-up to the war; on the negotiations that took place in which each polity in Krepi was asked by Asante, Akwamu, and Anlo to decide whether or not they sought peace or were prepared to fight the invading forces; and on the invasion of Ho, see Hornberger, "Völlingen Zerstörung," 1006.

46. The people of Ho were not the only ones subject to these kinds of actions. So, too, were their allies, the people of Agotime. When eighteen Agotime citizens sought refuge in the polity of Agu, for example, they were promptly handed over to the Asantes. Eight of the eighteen were killed immediately. The remaining ten were enslaved. "Es war unsere Hoffnung," 1016.

47. On the Ho agricultural calendar, see Spieth, *Ewe*, 358–59.

48. Spieth, *Ewe*, 110–12. This quote comes from Greene, *West African Narratives*, 87.

49. No reports describe the outbreak of disease specifically among the Ho troops, but NDMG accounts indicate that such outbreaks did emerge among the Ho polity's allies as well as among the Asantes and Anlos. From this, we can assume that the people of Ho suffered the same as they followed their troops through the region. See "Der Krieg" (20, no. 233 [1870]): 1044; "Es war unsere Hoffnung," 1016.

50. Reports of looting in the various towns through which the Asante, Anlo, and Akwamu passed indicate what kinds of items the invading forces sought. See Hornberger, "Völlingen Zerstörung," 1006; Merz, "Waya" (21, no. 251 [1871]): 1130; J. Illg and J. Müller, "Der Ashanti Krieg," 1009; Merz, "Die Ashanteer in Waya," 1077–78; Binder, "Verhandlungen wegen Waya," 1117.

51. Merz, "Waya" (21, no. 251 [1871]): 1130. Just as the people in Krepi were in great debt because of the war, so, too, were the Anlo. They had provided a great quantity of firearms and gunpowder to the Asantes for the war and had expected to receive prisoners of war whom they could enslave as payment from the Asantes. This payment, however, was never forthcoming as the Asantes failed to capture as many in Agotime as they hoped and, as the war continued, their desire to keep as many prisoners as possible for themselves meant that when Asante attacked its own allies in the region (Wusuta, for example, as well as Sokode) they took them as prisoners back to Kumase rather than handing them over to the Anlo. See J. Illg and J. Müller, "Der Ashanti Krieg," 1011; and Merz, "Waya" (21, no. 251 [1871]): 1130. Indebtedness came not just as a result of the war, however. The business situation in the interior and on the coast, both before and after the war, resulted in heavy indebtedness. See Greene, *Gender*, 102–4; Haenger, *Slaves and Slave Holders*, 69–73; Binetsch, "Aus Ho," 188–89.

52. "Aus dem Innern," 1207–8.

53. Bremen Staatsarchiv: 7, 1025–12/2: Letter from Stephan Kwami, Ho Mission House, to Bremen Mission, 14 April 1883.

54. Spieth, *Ewe*, 120.

55. See Greene, *West African Narratives*, 87–88 and 104–5, for a more detailed chronology of Asante's actions in Taviefe, which were not unique. It did the same in Wusuta, Waya, Adaklu, and Sokode. On Asante behavior in Wusuta, see Greene, *West African Narratives*, 124–25; on Asante behavior in Waya, see J. Illg and J. Müller, "Der Ashanti Krieg," 1010, and "Der Afrikanische Krieg," 1070; on Asante behavior in both Waya and Adaklu, see Merz, "Die Ashanteer in Waya," 1077; on Asante behavior in Sokode, see Spieth, *Ewe*, 108.

56. "Noah Yawo," 332–33.

57. "Noah Yawo," 332; for a discussion of some of the talismans (or charms as Spieth calls them), that were popular in Ho at the time he was working in the area (1880–1902), see Spieth, *Ewe*, 544–46 and 553–55.

58. In a report written in 1875 about Hornberger's 1862 speech, the missionaries used their knowledge about the smallpox epidemic and the war that followed the earthquake to alter his words. They claimed that Hornberger did not just speak of stronger earthquakes and terribly hard times to come, but rather cited specifically pestilence and war, the very events that did follow the earthquake. They did so, presumably, to reinforce for their German readers, the power of the Bible to predict the future for those who fail to convert or take seriously their Christian faith. See "Noah Yawo," 333.

59. Müller, *Geschichte*, 177, 178.

60. "Noah Yawo," 329.

61. The notion that the Christian God was more powerful than any local deity was the way most Ewe-speaking peoples in West Africa made sense of Christianity. They continued to believe in the power of other spiritual forces. God, the Christian God, was just much more powerful.

62. These nineteenth-century socialization norms are most evident in the proverbs that Spieth collected in the seventeen years he lived and worked in Ho, beginning in 1880. See Spieth, *Ewe*, 619–33, esp. proverbs 1, 2, 19, 47, 49, 63, 65, and 105.

63. "Noah Yawo," 333.

64. Müller, *Geschichte*, 176. See also Greene, *West African Narratives*, 105, for a more precise chronology of the different visits made to Ho by those affiliated with the NDMG.

65. "Noah Yawo," 33.

66. R. Illg, "Was Frau Illg von Ho erzällt," 408–9.

67. Noah Yawo's conversion to Christianity, as well as the earlier conversion of Tenu Kwami, was considered by the NDMG missionaries to be a major turning point in their efforts to bring the people of Ho to their faith. Prior to this, most of the Africans who lived in Ho as Christians were not citizens of the town, and were either former slaves or individuals who came from families that had long been associated with various European traders on the coast. The status of Tenu and Yawo as respected local priest and prominent local leader respectively, kindled the missionaries' hopes that their positions in Ho would encourage others to convert to Christianity as well.

68. On the many changes demanded by the NDMG missionaries of their converts, including their ethnic identity, clothing, music, burial practices, etc., see Greene, *Sacred Sites.*

69. "Noah Yawo," 333–34; "Noch einmal Ho," 10; Müller, *Geschichte,* 179.

70. This set of funeral rituals was appropriate for adult men and women as well as for children in Ho during the mid-to-late nineteenth century. Somewhat different rituals accompanied the funerals of infants, local priests, and those who died in war. For descriptions of these different funeral practices, see Spieth, *Ewe,* 304–44.

71. On NDMG understandings of proper funerary practices, see S. Spiess, "Heidnische und Christliche," 6–8; on the objections the African Christians in Ho had to participating in local funerary practices, see Bremen Staatsarchiv: 7, 1025–12/2: Letter from Josef Reindorf, Ho, to the Inspector, 5 February 1877.

72. Bremen Staatsarchiv: 7, 1025–12/2: Letter from Josef Reindorf, Ho, to the Inspector, 5 February 1877; see also Bremen Staatsarchiv: 7, 1025–12/2: Letter from Joseph Reindorf to Gentlemen, 10 July 1875.

73. On Lydia's life, see Greene, *West African Narratives,* pt. 2.

74. Spieth, *Ewe,* 331.

75. According to Spieth, *Ewe,* 248, this fine in the late nineteenth century was usually the cost of seven human beings: eight hundred *hotu.* The person who accidentally shot and killed someone was also expected to provide a woman to the family of the deceased as part of the compensation. Nothing is said about this, however, in the account about Isaak and the negotiations that followed his accidental killing of Mose Dake.

76. When Noah Yawo decided to convert to Christianity, all his wives were quite opposed to the idea. Two of them left him, although they agreed to marry others in his family. As adult women, the decision was theirs although they may have been heavily influenced by their families. For younger women, their families would have been even more involved. See also Mallet, "Briefe," 137.

77. "Noch einmal Ho," 11.

78. "Noah Yawo," 334.

79. R. Illg, "Was Frau Illg von Ho erzällt," 404–10.

80. See "Aus dem Innern," 1208. On when safer travel became possible, see Greene, *West African Narratives,* 238n27.

81. "Noch einmal Ho," 10.

82. This notion that the Christian God was more powerful than local gods and spirits is discussed fully in Meyer, *Translating the Devil.*

83. Bremen Staatsarchiv: 7, 1025–12/2: Letter from Joseph Reindorf to Gentlemen, 10 July 1875; "Noch einmal Ho," 10. The amenities not normally found in local homes included large windows and a well-constructed and spacious bathroom. See R. Illg, "Was Frau Illg von Ho erzällt," 409. On the usual placement of bathrooms, see Spieth, *Ewe,* 284.

84. On the Basel Mission and its position on slavery, see Haenger, *Slaves and Slave Holders*, 15–24. On the close ties between the Basel Mission and the NDMG, see Knoll, *Togo*, 16, 96–97; and Meyer, *Translating the Devil*, 29.

85. Ustorf, *Bremen Missionaries*, 282.

86. In Greene, *West African Narratives*, 105, I indicated that Noah freed his slaves when he was baptized in 1873. That was not the case. Debrunner, *Church*, 97, is also incorrect in stating he freed his slaves in 1874. In a letter to the NDMG Inspector, dated 5 February 1877, Josef Reindorf indicated that only at that time did Noah free his last slave. See Bremen Staatsarchiv: 7, 1025–12/2: Letter from Josef Reindorf, Ho, to the Inspector, 5 February 1877.

87. In 1883 Noah had the title of presbyter (elder). He demonstrated his devotion to the work of the church by accompanying Stephen Kwami on a preaching tour to Taviefe, Matse, Tanyigbe, and Akoviefe. That the European missionaries as well as their African assistants wrote so much about Noah is also evidence of his attachment to the NDMG and the regard that those associated with the mission had for him. Bremen Staatsarchiv: 7, 1025–12/2: Letter from Stephen Kwami, Ho Mission House, to Reverends and dear Gentlemen, 14 April 1883.

88. "Ein Fetisch Priester," 63.

89. On the educational background and business interests of some of these teachers and catechists, see Bühler, "Volta Region," 66–69, 75–81.

90. On the difficulty the people of Krepi had in getting goods to Accra during this period, see Asare, "Akwamu-Peki Relations," 97–99.

91. Peace between Ho and its enemies was finally reestablished in 1884. See Greene, *West African Narratives*, 38–39.

92. The establishment of the permanent station with Rudolph Mallet as its designated minister occurred in 1881. Debrunner, *Church*, 97.

93. Examples of such efforts in the Krepi region can be found in Bremen Staatsarchiv: 7, 1025–12/2: Briefe von Lehrern in Englisher Sprache, 18 June 1884. This letter was republished under the title "Kpengoe, 18 Juni 1884"; see Mallet, "Briefe," 137–38.

94. For a discussion of British efforts to contain the hostilities that still simmered because of the 1869–71 war, see Herold, Die politische Vergangenheit," 122–27.

95. Knoll, *Togo*, 17–36; and Bühler, "Volta Region," 125–76.

96. Maier, "Slave Labor," 74. As noted by Maier, German colonial officials did not have the manpower to enforce abolition, but their interests were also elsewhere, on making the colony pay for its own administration. A similar situation existed in East Africa, although abolition came even later there. See Deutsch, *Emancipation*.

97. Amenumey, "German Administration," 626.

98. Johnson, "Slaves," 355.

99. Johnson, "Slaves," 345–55; Deutsch and Zeuske, "Slavery." It should be noted that they not only did nothing to end the buying, selling, and retention of enslaved peoples who had been captured in war or kidnapped, they actually legalized debt bondage, and implemented a system of unpaid forced labor. Maier, "Slave Labor," 75–88.

100. See Austin, *Labour*, 203–49, on the demise of slavery (including debt slavery) in Ghana as wage labor emerged, although this shift occurred at different times for men and women; for specifics on the transition from slave to free labor in Krepe, see Brydon, "After Slavery."

101. On the use of forced labor by the colonial government or its agents (chiefs, in particular) in Ghana, see Austin, *Labour*, 217–20; and Dumett, *El Dorado*, 150. For an overview of the literature on forced labor and protests about it as slavery in West Africa, see Cooper, "Conditions," Ash, "Forced Labor," and Whyte, "Freedom." On the role of the newly independent Ghana government in protesting the use of forced labor in Angola, see Ball, "Colonial Labor," 6.

102. On local African criticisms of slavery as cruel, see Greene, "Minority Voices."

103. That the acceptance of such ideas is now quite widespread is evident in local reactions in Ghana to the discovery of old forms of religious slavery that have continued to exist in certain parts of the country, as well as responses to new forms that have been discovered in the late twentieth and twenty-first century in the Volta Lake fishing industry. On Ghanaian responses to these, see British Council, *Securing the Inalienable Rights*; Hamenoo and Sottie, "Stories"; and Agbenya, "Child Labour Trafficking."

4. Concluding Thoughts

1. There is an enormous body of literature that explores the factors that influenced the decisions made by various political, judicial, economic, and religious leaders. Some of this literature, especially that on foreign policy decision making, has been generated by political scientists. These studies, however, have greatly influenced historical studies. For a concise and readable summary of studies on U.S. foreign policy decision making, see Houghton, *Decision Point*. See also Minz and DeRouen Jr., *Understanding*. Another important political science study on decision making is by Jervis, *Perception and Misperception*. Jervis's study is central to Granville's historical study, *The First Domino*. A study that makes U.S. Supreme Court judicial decision making central to its analysis is Silverstein's, *Constitutional Faiths*. Among the studies that have sought to understand both the societal and personal influences on the decisions of slave owners in terms of how they handled their enslaved property, see recent studies by Schafer, *Zephaniah Kingsley Jr.*, and Burnard, *Mastery, Tyranny and Desire*. On the factors that are said to have influenced Lincoln's decision to emancipate the slaves in rebel territories, see Miller, *Lincoln and Leadership*.

2. On the notion that peer pressure, or group think, influences decisions, see Janis, *Victims of Groupthink* as well as recent reassessment of Janis' classic study by Schafer and Crichlow, *Groupthink vs. High-Quality Decision Making*.

3. For a discussion of the history of the movement to free the *trokosis*, see Ameh, "Reconciling Human Rights."

4. On the problem of slavery in the Lake Volta fisheries, see Agbenya, "Child Labour Trafficking," and Hamenoo and Sottie, "Stories." On the Village of Hope and the Christian values that guide its work, see http://www.thevillageofhope.com/, accessed 15 April 2015.

5. On the antislavery movements in Muslim majority areas in West Africa, see Lecocq, "Bellah Question," and Hahonou and Pelckmans, "West African Antislavery Movements." On the use of Islamic rhetoric to counter old hierarchies, see Gaibazzi, "Moving Out."

Bibliography

Books and Articles

Abun-Nasr, Sonia. *Afrikaner und Missionar: Die Lebensgeschichte von David Asante.* Basel: Schelettwein, 2003.

———. "David Asante." In *Dictionary of African Biography,* edited by Henry Louis Gates Jr. and Emmanuel Akyeampong. Oxford African American Studies Center, http://www.oxfordaasc.com/article/opr/t338/e0209. Accessed 16 January 2014.

Achebe, Nwando. *The Female King of Colonial Nigeria: Ahebi Ugbabe.* Bloomington: Indiana University Press, 2011.

Addo-Fening, Robert. *Akyem-Abuakwa, 1700–1943: From Ofori Panin to Sir Ofori Atta.* Trondheim: Dept. of History, Norwegian University of Science and Technology, 2001.

"Ein Aergerlicher Auftritt." *Monatsblatt der Norddeutschen Missions-Gesellschaft* 21, no. 247 (1871): 1112.

Agbodeka, Francis. *African Politics and British Policy in the Gold Coast, 1868–1900: A Study in the Forms and Force of Protest.* London: Longman, 1971.

Akurang-Parry, Kwabena O. "A Smattering of Education" and Petitions as Sources: A Study of African Slaveholders' Responses to Abolition in the Gold Coast Colony, 1874–1875." *History in Africa* 27 (2000): 39–60.

———. "We Shall Rejoice to See the Day When Slavery Shall Cease to Exist": The *Gold Coast Times,* the African Intelligentsia, and Abolition in the Gold Coast. *History in Africa* 31 (2004): 19–42.

Akyeampong, Emmanuel Kwaku. *Between the Sea and the Lagoon: An Eco-Social History of the Anlo of Southeastern Ghana, c. 1850 to Recent Times.* Athens: Ohio University Press, 2001.

Allman, Jean, ed. *Fashioning Africa: Power and the Politics of Dress.* Bloomington: Indiana University Press, 2004.

"Ein Alter Heide." *Monatsblatt der Norddeutschen Missions-Gesellschaft* 5 (Mai, 1888): 80–84.

Ameh, Robert Kwame. "Reconciling Human Rights and Traditional Practices: The Anti-*Trokosi* Campaign in Ghana." *Canadian Journal of Law and Society* 19, no. 2 (2004): 51–72.

Amenumey, D. E. K. "German Administration in Southern Togo." *Journal of African History* 10, no. 4 (1969): 623–39.

American Anthropological Association. "Principles of Professional Responsibility," 1 November 2012. http://ethics.aaanet.org/category/statement/. Accessed 3 March 2015.

American Historical Association. *Statement of Standards of Professional Conduct.* Washington D.C.: American Historical Association, 2011.

Ash, Catherine B. "Forced Labor in Colonial West Africa." *History Compass* 4, no. 3 (2006): 402–6.

"Aus dem Innern: Etwas von der Politik." *Monatsblatt der Norddeutschen Missions-Gesellschaft* 23, no. 266 (1873): 1202–8.

Austin, Gareth. *Labour, Land and Capital in Ghana: From Slavery to Free Labour in Asante, 1807–1956*. Rochester, N.Y.: University of Rochester Press, 2005.

Awoonor, Kofi. *Guardians of the Sacred Word: Ewe Poetry*. New York: Nok Publishers, 1974.

Ayandele, E. A. *Holy Johnson: Pioneer of African Nationalism, 1836–1917*. New York: Humanities Press, 1970.

Backscheider, Paula. *Reflections on Biography*. Oxford: Oxford University Press, 1999.

Ball, Jeremy. "Colonial Labor in Twentieth-Century Angola." *History Compass* 3, no. 1 (2005): 1–9.

Bellagamba, Alice. "Reasons for Silence: Tracing the Legacy of Internal Slavery and Slave Trade in Contemporary Gambia." In *Politics of Memory: Making Slavery Visible in the Public Space*, edited by Ana Lucia Araujo, 35–53. New York: Routledge, 2012.

———. "The Legacies of Slavery in southern Senegal." Https://www.opendemocracy .net/beyondslavery/alice-bellagamba/legacies-of-slavery-in-southern-senegal. Accessed 1 May 2015.

Bellagamba, Alice, Sandra E. Greene and Martin A. Klein, eds. *African Voices on Slavery and the Slave Trade*. Cambridge: Cambridge University Press, 2013.

———. *The Bitter Legacy: African Slavery Past and Present*. Princeton: Markus Wiener, 2013.

Binder, Johann Conrad. "Verhandlungen wegen Waya." *Monatsblatt der Norddeutschen Missions-Gesellschaft* 21, no. 247 (1871): 1112–13.

Binetsch, Gottlob. "Aus Ho." *Monatsblatt der Norddeutschen Missions-Gesellschaft* 12 (1880): 188–89.

Botte, Roger, ed. *Esclavage moderne ou modernité de l'esclavage?* Special issue, *Cahiers d'Étude africaines* 179–180 (2005).

———, ed. *L'ombre portée de l'esclavage: Avatars contemporains de l'oppression sociale*. Special issue, *Journal des africanistes* 70, nos. 1–2 (2000).

———. "Riimayɓe, Ḥarāṭīn, Iklan: Les damnés de la terre, le développement et la démocratie." In *Horizons nomades en Afrique sahélienne: Sociétés, développement et démocratie*, edited by André Bourgeot, 55–78. Paris: Karthala, 1999.

Bouché, Pierre. *La Côte des ésclaves et le Dahomey*. Paris: E. Plon, Nourrit, 1885.

British Council. *Securing the Inalienable Rights of Women and Children in Trokosi Bondage*. Accra: British Council, 1998.

Brivio, Alessandra. "Evoking the Past through Material Culture: The Mami Tchamba Shrine." In Bellagamba, Greene, and Klein, *Bitter Legacy*, 149–62.

Brooks, George E. *Landlords and Strangers: Ecology, Society and Trade in Western Africa, 1000–1630*. Boulder, Colo.: Westview Press, 1993.

———. "A Nhara of the Guinea-Bissau Region: Mãe Aurélia Correia." In *Women and Slavery in Africa*, edited by Claire C. Robertson and Martin A. Klein, 295–319. Madison: University of Wisconsin Press, 1983.

———. "The Signares of Saint-Louis and Gorée: Women Entrepreneurs in Eighteenth-Century Senegal." In *Women in Africa: Studies in Social and Economic Change*, edited by Nancy J. Hafkin and Edna G. Bay, 19–44. Stanford, Calif.: Stanford University Press, 1976.

Brown, Carolyn A. "Testing the Boundaries of Marginality: Twentieth-Century Slavery and Emancipation Struggles in Nkanu, Northern Igboland, 1920–29." *Journal of African History* 37, no. 1 (1996): 51–80.

Brown, Christopher Leslie. *Moral Capital: Foundations of British Abolitionism.* Chapel Hill: University of North Carolina Press, 2006.

Brydon, Lynne. "After Slavery, What Next? Productive Relations in Early Twentieth-Century Krepe, and Beyond." In *The Changing Worlds of Atlantic Africa: Essays in Honor of Robin Law,* edited by Toyin Falola and Matt D. Childs, 479–95. Durham, N.C.: Carolina Academic Press, 2009.

Bürgi, E. "Sammlung von Ewe-Sprichwörtern." *Archiv für Anthropologie (Braunschweig),* N.F., Bd. 13 (1915): 415–50.

Burnard, Trevor. *Mastery, Tyranny and Desire: Thomas Thistlewood and His Slaves in the Anglo-Jamaican World.* Chapel Hill: University of North Carolina Press, 2004.

Byfield, Judith. "Dress and Politics in Post–World War II Abeokuta (Western Nigeria)." In Allman, *Fashioning Africa,* 31–49.

Cassanelli, Lee V. "The Ending of Slavery in Italian Somalia: Liberty and the Control of Labor, 1890–1935." In Miers and Roberts, *End of Slavery,* 308–31.

Cookey, S. J. S. *King Jaja of the Niger Delta: His Life and Times, 1821–1891.* New York: NOK, 1974.

Cooper, Frederick. "Conflict and Connection: Rethinking Colonial African History." *American Historical Review* 99, no. 5 (1994): 1516–45.

———. "Conditions Analogous to Slavery: Imperialism and Free Labor Ideology in Africa." In *Beyond Slavery: Explorations of Race, Labor, and Citizenship in Post-emancipation Societies,* edited by Frederick Cooper, Thomas C. Holt, and Rebecca J. Scott, 130–43. Chapel Hill: University of North Carolina Press, 2000.

Crais, Clifton. "Resistance and Accommodation." In *New Dictionary of the History of Ideas, Volume 5,* edited by Maryanne Cline Horowitz, 2106–10. Detroit: Thomas Gale, 2005.

Darnton, Robert. "Looking the Devil in the Face." *New York Review of Books,* 10 February 2000. Accessed 5 September 2012. http://www.nybooks.com/articles /archives/2000/feb/10.

de Bruijn, Mirjam, and Lotte Pelckmans. "Facing Dilemmas: Former Fulbe Slaves in Modern Mali." *Canadian Journal of African Studies* 39, no. 1 (2005): 69–95.

Debrunner, Hans W. *A Church Between Colonial Powers: A Study of the Church in Togo.* Translated by Dorothea M. Barton. London: Lutterworth Press, 1965.

Deutsch, Jan-Georg. *Emancipation without Abolition in German East Africa, c. 1884–1914.* Oxford: James Currey, 2006.

Deutsch, Jan-Georg, and Michael Zeuske. "Slavery, the Slave Trade and Abolition." In *A Historical Companion to Postcolonial Literatures: Continental Europe and Its Empires,* edited by Prem Poddar, Rajeev S. Patke, and Lars Jensen, 252–54. Edinburgh: Edinburgh University Press, 2008.

Dike, Kenneth Onwuka. *Trade and Politics in the Niger Delta, 1830–1885:* An Introduction to the Economic and Political History of Nigeria. Oxford: Clarendon Press, 1956.

Doortmont, Michel R. *The Pen-Pictures of Modern Africans and African Celebrities by Charles Francis Hutchinson: A Collective Biography of Elite Society in the Gold Coast Colony.* Leiden: Brill, 2005.

Duffy, Helen. *"Hadijatou Mani Koroua v Niger*: Slavery Unveiled by the ECOWAS Court." *Human Rights Law Review* 9, no. 1 (2009): 151–70.

Dumett, Raymond. *El Dorado in West Africa: The Gold Coast Mining Frontier, African Labor and Colonial Capitalism in the Gold Coast, 1875–1900.* Athens: Ohio University Press, 1998.

"Es war unsere Hoffnung." *Monats-Blatt der Norddeutschen Missionsgesellschaft* 19, 227 (1869) 1016.

Falola, Toyin. "Efusetan Aniwura of Ibaden (1820s–1874): A Woman Who Rose to the Rank of a Chief but Whom Male Rivals Destroyed." In *The Human Tradition in Modern Africa*, edited by Dennis D. Cordell, 31–36. Lanham, MD: Rowman and Littlefield, 2012.

"Ein Fetisch Priester." *Der Mission-Freund* 19, no. 4 (1864): 49–64.

Fynn, J. K. *Asante and Its Neighbors, 1700–1807.* London: Longman, 1971.

Gaibazzi, Paolo. "Moving Out, Moving Up?: Slavery and Migration among the Soninke of the Upper Gambia Basin." Paper presented at the conference on Tales of Slavery: Narratives of Slavery, the Slave Trade and Enslavement in Africa, University of Toronto, May 2009.

Geary, Christraud M. "Missionary Photography: Private and Public Readings." In "Historical Photography of Africa," edited by Marla C. Berns, Allen F. Roberts, Mary Nooter Roberts, Gemma Rodrigues, and Doran H. Ross, special issue, *African Arts* 24, no. 4 (1991): 48–59, 98–100.

Getz, Trevor. "The Case for Africans: The Role of Slaves and Masters in Emancipation on the Gold Coast, 1874–1900." *Slavery and Abolition* 21, no. 1 (2000): 128–45.

Gold Coast and Stanley William Morgan. *The Gold Coast Civil Service List, 1898.* London: Waterlow and Sons, 1898–1931.

Granville, Johanna C. *The First Domino: International Decision Making during the Hungarian Crisis of 1956.* College Station: Texas A&M University Press, 2004.

Greene, Sandra E. "Crossing Boundaries/Changing Identities: Female Slaves, Male Strangers, and Their Descendants in Nineteenth- and Twentieth-Century Anlo." In *Gendered Encounters: Challenging Cultural Boundaries and Social Hierarchies in Africa*, edited by Maria Grosz-Ngaté and Omari H. Kokole, 23–42. New York: Routledge, 1997.

———. *Gender, Ethnicity, and Social Change on the Upper Slave Coast: A History of the Anlo-Ewe.* Portsmouth, N.H.: Heinemann, 1996.

———. "Minority Voices: Abolitionism in West Africa." *Slavery and Abolition*, 23 February 2015, http://www.tandfonline.com/doi/abs/10.1080/0144039X.2015.1008213#, DOI: 10.1080/0144039X.2015.1008213.

———. *Sacred Sites and the Colonial Encounter: A History of Meaning and Memory in Ghana.* Bloomington: Indiana University Press, 2002.

———. *West African Narratives of Slavery: Texts from Nineteenth- and Early Twentieth-Century Ghana.* Bloomington: Indiana University Press, 2011.

———. "Whispers and Silences: Explorations in African Oral History." *Africa Today* 50, no. 2 (2003): 41–53.

Haenger, Peter. *Slaves and Slave Holders on the Gold Coast: Towards an Understanding of Social Bondage in West Africa.* Basel: P. Schlettwein, 2000.

Hahonou, Eric K., "Past and Present African Citizenships of Slave Descent: Lessons from Benin." *Citizenship Studies* 15, no. 1 (2011): 75–92.

———. "Slavery and Politics: Stigma, Decentralisation and Political Representation in Niger and Benin," in Rossi, *Reconfiguring Slavery,* 152–81.

Hahonou, Eric K., and Lotte Pelckmans, "West African Antislavery Movements: Citizenship Struggles and the Legacies of Slavery." *Stichproben: Wiener Zeitschrift für kritische Afrikastudien* 20 (2011): 141–62.

Hall, Bruce. *A History of Race in Muslim West Africa, 1600–1960.* Cambridge: Cambridge University Press, 2011.

Hamenoo, Emma Seyram, and Cynthia Akorfa Sottie. "Stories from Lake Volta: The Lived Experiences of Trafficked Children in Ghana." *Child Abuse & Neglect* 40 (2015): 103–12.

Hardung, Christine. "Curse and Blessing: On Post-Slavery Modes of Perception and Agency in Benin." In Rossi, *Reconfiguring Slavery,* 116–39.

Hay, Margaret Jean. "Changes in Clothing and Struggles over Identity in Colonial Western Kenya." In Allman, *Fashioning Africa,* 67–83.

Herold, Premierlieutenant. "Die politische vergangenheit des westlichen Togo-Gebietes." *Mittheilungen von Forschungsreisenden und Gelehrten aus den Deutschen Schutzgebieten* 4 (1891): 113–27.

Hiskett, Mervyn. *The Sword of Truth: The Life and Times of the Shehu Usuman dan Fodio.* New York: Oxford University Press, 1973.

Hogendorn, J. S., and Paul E. Lovejoy. "The Reform of Slavery in Early Colonial Nigeria." In Miers and Roberts, *End of Slavery,* 391–414.

Holsey, Bayo. "Owning Up to the Past?: African Slave Traders and the Hazards of Discourse." *Transition* 105 (2011): 74–87.

———. *Routes of Remembrance: Refashioning the Slave Trade in Ghana.* Chicago: University of Chicago Press, 2008.

———. "Writing about the Slave Trade: Early-Twentieth-Century Colonial Textbooks and their Authors." In Bellagamba, Greene and Klein, *African Voices,* 204–9.

Hornberger, Christian. "Etwas aus der Geschichte der Anloer." *Quartal-Blatt der Norddeutschen Missions-Gesellschaft* 82, (Marz, 1877): 436–66.

———. "Fetischwesen in Wegbe." *Monatsblatt der Norddeutschen Missions-Gesellschaft* 14, no. 166 (1864): 731.

———. "Neger-Doctoren." *Monatsblatt der Norddeutschen Missions-Gesellschaft.* Supplement to issue no. 285 (1874): no page numbers indicated.

———. Untitled. *Monatsblatt der Norddeutschen Missions-Gesellschaft* 14, no. 157 (1864): 685–89.

———. "Völlingen Zerstörung unsrer Station Wegbe." *Monatsblatt der Norddeutschen Missions-Gesellschaft* 19, no. 225 (1869): 1006.

———. "Wegbe." *Monatsblatt der Norddeutschen Missions-Gesellschaft* 12, no. 142 (1862): 619–20.

———. "Wegbe." *Monatsblatt der Norddeutschen Missions-Gesellschaft* 11, no. 125 (1861): 570.

Horton, Africanus B. *Letters on the Political Condition of the Gold Coast . . .* London: W. J. Johnson, 1970. First published 1870 by Frank Cass.

Horton, Robin. "From Fishing Village to City-State: A Social History of New Calabar." In *Man in Africa*, edited by Phyllis M. Kaberry and Mary Douglas, 37–58. London: Tavistock, 1969.

Houghton, David Patrick. *The Decision Point: Six Cases in U.S. Foreign Policy Decision Making*. New York: Oxford University Press, 2013.

Illg, J. D., and J. Jakob Müller. "Der Afrikanische Krieg." *Monatsblatt der Norddeutschen Missions-Gesellschaft* 20, no. 238 (1870): 1070–72.

———. "Der Ashanti Krieg." *Monatsblatt der Norddeutschen Missions-Gesellschaft* 19, no. 226 (1869): 1009–11.

Illg, R. "Was Frau Illg von Ho erzählt." *Quartal-Blatt der Norddeutschen Missions-Gesellschaft* 74 (1875): 404–10.

Ipsen, Pernille. *Daughters of the Trade: Atlantic Slavers and Interracial Marriage on the Gold Coast*. Philadelphia: University of Pennsylvania Press, 2015.

Janis, Irving. *Victims of Group Think: A Psychological Study of Foreign-Policy Decisions and Fiascos*. Boston: Houghton Mifflin, 1972.

Jeanne, Matthieu. "La mise en scène de l'esclavage dans l'espace saharo-sahélien: Discours, actions et profits de l'association Timidria au Niger." *Oriental Archive* 80, no. 2 (2012): 191–206.

Jervis, Robert. *Perception and Misperception in International Politics*. Princeton: Princeton University Press, 1976.

Johnson, Marion. "Ashanti East of the Volta." *Transactions of the Historical Society of Ghana* 8 (1965): 33–59.

———. "The Cowrie Currencies of West Africa, Part I." *Journal of African History* XI, 1 (1970): 17–49.

———. "The Cowrie Currencies of West Africa, Part II." *Journal of African History*, XI, 3 (1970): 331–53.

———. "The Slaves of Salaga." *Journal of African History* 27, no. 2 (1986): 341–62.

Johnson, Michael P., and James L. Roark. *Black Masters: A Free Family of Color in the Old South*. New York: Norton, 1984.

Jones, G. I. *The Trading States of the Oil Rivers: A Study of Political Development in Eastern Nigeria*. London: Oxford University Press, 1963.

Kea, R. A. "Akwamu-Anlo Relations, c. 1750–1813." *Transactions of the Historical Society of Ghana* 10 (1969): 29–63.

Klein, Martin A. *Slavery and Colonial Rule in French West Africa*. Cambridge: Cambridge University Press, 1998.

Knoll, Arthur J. *Togo under Imperial Germany, 1884–1914*. Stanford, Calif.: Hoover Institution Press, 1978.

Koger, Larry. *Black Slaveowners: Free Black Slave Masters in South Carolina, 1790–1860* Jefferson, NC: Mcfarland, 1985.

"Der Krieg." *Monatsblatt der Norddeutschen Missions-Gesellschaft* 20, no. 229 (1870): 1030.

"Der Krieg." *Monatsblatt der Norddeutschen Missions-Gesellschaft* 20, no. 231 (1870): 1036–37.

"Der Krieg." *Monatsblatt der Norddeutschen Missions-Gesellschaft* 20, no. 232 (1870): 1039–40.

"Der Krieg." *Monatsblatt der Norddeutschen Missions-Gesellschaft* 20, no. 233 (1870): 1044–45.

"Kriegsnachrichten aus Afrika." *Monatsblatt der Norddeutschen Missions-Gesellschaft* 19, no. 223 (1869): 995–97.

Larson, Pier M. "Slaving in Africa." In *The Princeton Companion to Atlantic History*, edited by Joseph C. Miller, 425–29. Princeton: Princeton University Press, 2015.

Law, Robin. "Computing Domestic Prices in Precolonial West Africa: A Methodological Exercise from the Slave Coast." *History in Africa* 18 (1991): 239–57.

Lecocq, Baz. "The Bellah Question: Slave Emancipation, Race, and Social Categories in Late Twentieth Century Northern Mali." *Canadian Journal of African Studies* 39, no. 1 (2005): 42–68.

Lovejoy. Paul E., ed. *The Ideology of Slavery in Africa*. Beverly Hills: Sage Publications, 1981.

Maier, Donna J. E. "Asante War Aims in the 1869 Invasion of Ewe." In *The Golden Stool: Studies of the Asante Center and Periphery*, edited by Enid Schildkrout, 232–44. New York: American Museum of Natural History, 1987.

———. "Slave Labor and Wage Labor in German Togo, 1885–1914." In *Germans in the Tropics: Essays in German Colonial History*, edited by Arthur J. Knoll and Lewis H. Gann, 73–92. New York: Greenwood Press, 1987.

Mallet, Rudolph. "Briefe eines Neger-Pastors, Kpengoe, 18 Juni 1884." *Monatsblatt der Norddeutschen Missions-Gesellschaft* 9, no. 9 (1884): 137–38.

Mann, Kristin. *Slavery and the Birth of an African City: Lagos, 1760–1900*. Bloomington: Indiana University Press, 2007.

McDougall, E. Ann. "Living the Legacy of Slavery Between Discourse and Reality." *Cahiers d'Études africaines* 179–180 (2005): 957–86.

Merz, Johannes. "Die Ashanteer in Waya." *Monatsblatt der Norddeutschen Missions-Gesellschaft* 20, 239 (1870): 1077–78.

———. *Ein Neger-Gehuelfe im Missionwerk: Das Leben das Katechisten Aaron Ony-ipayede* (Bremen: Buchdruckerei von C. Hilberloh, 1875).

———. "Ein trauriges Reiseerlebniss." *Monatsblatt der Norddeutschen Missions-Gesellschaft* 5, no. 1 (1876): 73–75.

———. "Waya." *Monatsblatt der Norddeutschen Missions-Gesellschaft* 20, no. 240 (1870): 1080–84.

———. "Waya," *Monatsblatt der Norddeutschen Missions-Gesellschaft* 21, 247 (1871): 1116–18.

———. "Waya." *Monatsblatt der Norddeutschen Missions-Gesellschaft* 21, 251 (1871): 1130.

Meyer, Birgit. *Translating the Devil: Religion and Modernity among the Ewe in Ghana*. Edinburgh: Edinburgh University Press, 1999.

Miers, Suzanne. "Slavery to Freedom in Sub-Saharan Africa: Expectations and Reality." In *After Slavery: Emancipation and Its Discontents*, edited by Howard Temperley, 237–64. London: Frank Cass, 2000.

Miers, Suzanne, and Richard Roberts, eds. *The End of Slavery in Africa*. Madison: University of Wisconsin Press, 1988.

Miller, Randall M., ed. *Lincoln and Leadership: Military, Political, and Religious Decision Making*. New York: Fordham University Press, 2012.

Minz, Alex, and Karel DeRouen, Jr. *Understanding Foreign Policy Decision Making.* New York: Cambridge University Press, 2010.

Müller, Gustav. *Geschichte der Ewe-Mission.* Bremen: Verlag der Norddeutschen Missions-Gesellschaft, 1904.

Nadel, Ira Bruce. *Biography: Fiction, Fact and Form.* New York: St. Martin's Press, 1984.

"Noah Yawo." *Quartal-Blatt der Norddeutschen Missions-Gesellschaft* 25, no. 293 (1875): 328–34.

"Noch Einmal Ho." *Monatsblatt der Norddeutschen Missions-Gesellschaft* 2, no. 1 (1877): 9–12.

Nørregård, Georg. *Danish Settlements in West Africa, 1658–1850.* Boston: Boston University Press, 1966.

Opata, Damian U. "On Remembering Slavery in Northern Igbo Proverbial Discourse." In Bellagamba, Greene, and Klein, *Bitter Legacy,* 57–65.

Parliamentary Papers, 1875: Correspondence relating to the Queen's Jurisdiction on the Gold Coast and the Abolition of Slavery within the Protectorate. London: Harrison and Sons, 1875.

Person, Yves. *Samori: Une révolution dyula.* 3 vols. Dakar: *L'Institute fundamental d'Afrique noire (IFAN)*: 1968–75.

Peterson, Brian J. "History, Memory and the Legacy of Samori in Southern Mali, c. 1800–1898." *Journal of African History* 49, no. 2 (2008): 261–79.

Rattray, R. S. *Ashanti Law and Constitution.* New York: Negro Universities Press, 1969. First published in 1911.

Reinke, E. F. "Eine Doppelfeier in Anloga." *Monatsblatt der Norddeutschen Missions-Gesellschaft* (Aug. 1914): 83–84.

Roberts, Richard. "The End of Slavery in the French Soudan, 1905–1914." In Miers and Roberts, *End of Slavery,* 282–307.

———. *Litigants and Households: African Disputes and Colonial Courts in the French Soudan, 1895–1912.* Portsmouth, N.H.: Heinemann, 2005.

Rossi, Benedetta. "Migration and Emancipation in West Africa's Labour History: The Missing Links." *Slavery and Abolition* 35, no. 1 (2014): 23–46.

———, ed. *Reconfiguring Slavery: West African Trajectories.* Liverpool: Liverpool University Press, 2009.

Runkel, Steffen. "The Perspectives of African Elites on Slavery and Abolition on the Gold Coast (1860–1900): Newspapers as Sources." In *Postcolonial Studies Across the Disciplines,* edited by Jana Gohrisch and Ellen Grünkemeier, 243–61. Amsterdam: Rodopi, 2013.

Saha, Zacharie. "Tabula and Pa Jacob: Two Twentieth-Century Slave Narratives from Cameroon." In Bellagamba, Greene, and Klein, *Bitter Legacy,* 119–31.

Salem, Zekeria Ould Ahmed. "Bare-Foot Activists: Transformations in the Haratine Movement in Mauretania." In *Movers and Shakers: Social Movements in Africa,* edited by Stephen Ellis and Ineke Van Kessel, 156–77. Leiden: Brill, 2009.

Schafer, Daniel L. *Zephaniah Kingsley Jr. and the Atlantic World: Slave Trader, Plantation Owner, Emancipator.* Gainesville: University Press of Florida, 2013.

Schafer, Mark and Scott Crichlow. *Groupthink vs. High-Quality Decision Making in International Relations.* New York: Columbia University Press, 2010.

Schiek, G. B. "Keta." *Monatsblatt der Norddeutschen Missions-Gesellschaft* 22, no. 263 (1872): 1193–94.

Schlegel, Bernhard. "Beitrag zur Geschichte, Welt- und Religionsanschauung des Westafrikaners namentlich der Eweers." *Monatsblatt der Norddeutschen Missions-Gesellschaft* 93, no. 7 (1858): 397–400, 406–8.

Schmitz, Jean. "Islamic Patronage and Republican Emancipation: The Slaves of the Al-maami in the Senegal River Valley." In Rossi, *Reconfiguring Slavery*, 85–115.

Schreiber, August W. *Bausteine zur Geschichte der Norddeutschen Missions-Gesellschaft.* Bremen: Verlag der Norddeutschen Missions-Gesellschaft, 1936.

Shopes, Linda. "Oral History, Human Subject and Institutional Review Boards." http://www.oralhistory.org/about/do-oral-history/oral-history-and-irb-review/. Accessed 6 March 2015.

Silverstein, Mark. *Constitutional Faiths: Felix Frankfurter, Hugo Black, and the Process of Judicial Decision Making.* Ithaca: Cornell University Press, 1984.

Sohne, William Godwin. *Genealogical Trees of the Quist, Amegashie and Allied Families and Abroad.* N.p.: 1992.

Spiess, Carl. "Bedeutung der Personennamen der Ewe-Neger in Westafrika." *Archiv für Anthropologie (Braunschweig)* 16 (1916): 104–59.

———. "Fünfzig Jahre Missionsarbeit in Anyako." *Monatsblatt der Norddeutschen Missions-Gesellschaft* (Jan. 1908): 3–6.

Spiess, Sophie. "Heidnische und Christliche Totenfeiern und Begräbnisse." *Quartal-Blatt der Norddeutschen Missions-Gesellschaft* 2 (1931): 6–8.

Spieth, Jakob. *The Ewe People: A Study of the Ewe People in German Togo.* Edited by Komla Amoaku. Berlin: Dietrich Reimer, 2011. First published in 1906.

Stilwell, Sean. *Paradoxes of Power: The Kano "Mamluks" and Male Royal Slavery in the Sokoto Caliphate, 1804–1903.* Portsmouth, N.H.: Heinemann, 2004.

Strickrodt, Silke. *Afro-European Trade in the Atlantic World: The Western Slave Coast, c1550–1885.* Woodbridge Suffolk: James Currey, 2015.

Surgy, Albert de. *La géomancie et le cult d'Afa chez les Evhé du littoral.* Paris: Publications orientalistes de France, 1981.

Tenkorang, S. "The Importance of Firearms in the Struggle between Ashanti and the Coastal States, 1708–1807." *Transactions of the Historical Society of Ghana* 9 (1968): 1–16.

Thioub, Ibrahima. "Regard critique sur les lectures africaines de l'esclavage et de la traite atlantique." In *Les historiens africaines et la mondialisation/African Historians and Globlization*, edited by Issiaka Mandé and Blandine Stefanson, 271–309. Paris: Karthala, 2005.

———. "Stigmas and Memory of Slavery in West Africa: Skin Color and Blood as Social Fracture Lines." *New Global Studies* 6, no. 3 (2012): article 4. DOI: 10.1515/1940–0004.1188.

Ustorf, Werner. *Bremen Missionaries in Togo and Ghana: 1847–1900.* Translated by James C. G. Greig. Accra: Asempa, 2002.

Valsecchi, Pierluigi. "'My Dearest Child Is My Slave's Child': Personal Status and the Politics of Succession in South-West Ghana (Nineteenth and Twentieth Centuries)." In *African Slaves, African Masters: Histories, Memories, Legacies*, edited by Alice Bellagamba, Sandra E. Greene, and Martin Klein. Trenton, N.J.: Africa World Press, forthcoming.

Weyhe, H. "Wegbe." *Monatsblatt der Norddeutschen Missions-Gesellschaft* 11, 128 (1861): 551.

"Wie man zu Anyako die Pocken vertreibt." *Quartalblatt der Norddeutschen Missions-Gesellschaft* 68 (1873): 321–24.

Wilks, Ivor G. *Asante in the Nineteenth Century: The Structure and Evolution of a Political Order.* Cambridge: Cambridge University Press, 1975.

Willis, John Ralph. *In the Path of Allah: The Passion of Al-Hajj 'Umar; An Essay into the Nature of Charisma in Islam.* London: Frank Cass, 1989.

Wright, Marcia. *Strategies of Slaves and Women: Life-Stories from East/Central Africa.* New York: Lillian Barber Press, 1993.

Zündel, Gottlob. "Afrika." *Monatsblatt der Norddeutschen Missions-Gesellschaft* 14, no. 183 (1866): 802–4.

Dissertations, Theses, Long Essays, and Unpublished Materials

Agbenya, Lillian. "Child Labour Trafficking in the Lake Volta Fishery of Ghana: A Case Study of Ogetse in the Krachi West District of the Volta Region." MA thesis, Department of Social and Marketing Studies, Norwegian College of Fishery Science, University of Tromsø, 2009.

Asare, E. B. "Akwamu-Peki Relations in the Eighteenth and Nineteenth Centuries." MA thesis, Institute of African Studies, University of Ghana, Legon, 1973.

Berndt, Jeremy Raphael. "Closer Than Your Jugular Vein: Muslim Intellectuals in a Malian Village, 1900 to the 1960s. PhD diss., Northwestern University, 2008.

Bühler, Peter. "The Volta Region of Ghana: Economic Change in Togoland, 1850–1914." PhD diss., University of California, San Diego, 1975.

Gaba, Kue Agbota. "The History of Anecho, Ancient and Modern." Unpublished manuscript. Deposited at Blame Library, University of Ghana, Legon, 1965.

Giraldo und der Kampf der Angloer gegen die Adaer. Document in the author's possession.

Gray, Natasha Adriene. "The Legal History of Witchcraft in Colonial Ghana: Akyem Abuakwa, 1913–1943." PhD diss., Columbia University, 2000.

Greene, Sandra E. "The Anlo-Ewe: Their Economy, Society and External Relations in the Eighteenth Century." PhD diss., Northwestern University, 1981.

Ocloo v. Amegashie and others. In the Supreme Court of the Gold Coast Colony held at Victoriaborg [*sic*], 17 August 1903, before his Honour, Sir W. Brandford Griffith, Chief Justice, 18–20. Court record in the possession of Togbi Amegashie IV, Accra-Nima.

Runkel, Steffen. "An African Abolitionist on the Gold Coast: The Case of Frances P. Fearon." Unpublished paper, 2015.

Sorkpor, Gershon A. "The Role of Awuna in the Triple Alliance Formed by Ashanti, Akwaku and Awuna during 1867–1874." MA seminar paper, Institute of African Studies, University of Ghana, Legon, 1966.

———. "Geraldo de Lima and the Awunas, 1862–1904." MA thesis. Institute of African Studies, University of Ghana, Legon, 1966.

Whyte, Christine. "Freedom but nothing else": The legacies of slavery and abolition in post-slavery Sierra Leone, 1928–1956." Paper delivered at University of Milan-Biccoca. Workshop on Shadows of Slavery in Africa and Beyond. May 2014.

Yarak, Larry. "Political Consolidation and Fragmentation in a Southern Akan Polity: Wassa and the Origin of Wassa Amenfi and Fiase, 1700–1840." Unpublished paper, 1976.

Yegbe, J. "The Anlo and Their Neighbors, 1850–1890." MA thesis, Institute of African Studies, University of Ghana, Legon, 1966.

Documents held by Christian Tamakloe, Keta. Accessed January 1988.
(a) Indenture, 11 October 1904.
(b) Agreement, between Avonokete and Avagashie of Jellacoffi on the one part and Chief Nyaho Tamakloe of Quittah on the other part.
(c) Agreement between King Amegbor and Chiefs and Headmen of Klikor and Chief Nyaho Tamakloe of Hutey.
(d) Indenture between George Briggance Wiliams of Freetown, Sierra Leone . . . and Chief Nyaho Tamaklo of Kwittah, 1902.
(e) Memorandum of Agreement between Thomas Wulff Cochrane of Acra and Chief Nyaho Tamakloe of Kwittah (and accompanying documents).
(f) Copy of Supreme Court case M. A. Williams v. Chief Tamakloe, 17 December 1906.
(g) Agreement between Chief N. Tamakloe of Keta and Messrs. Bodecker and Meyer, 31 May 1907.
(h) Copy of Judgment: Tetu Creek and Hillock, 7 November 1908.
(i) Native Court of Fia Sri II, Anloga: *Chief Tamakloe of Keta v. Klu Tsiamehia Lumo, Anyigblako Gbogbokuku of Dekpo*, 18 April 1910.

Newspapers and Periodicals

Africa Today
African Arts
American Historical Review
Archiv für Anthropologie (Braunschweig)
Cahiers d'Études africaines
Canadian Journal of African Studies
Canadian Journal of Law and Society
Child Abuse & Neglect
Citizenship Studies
History in Africa
History Compass
Human Rights Law Review
Journal of African History
Der Mission-Freund
Mittheilungen von Forschungsreisenden und Gelehrten aus den Deutschen Schutzgebieten
Monatsblatt der Norddeutschen Missions-Gesellschaft
New Global Studies
Quartal-Blatt der Norddeutschen Missions-Gesellschaft
Royal Gold Coast Gazette and Commercial Intelligencer

Slavery and Abolition
Stichproben: Wiener Zeitschrift für kritische Afrikastudien
Transactions of the Historical Society of Ghana
Transition

Websites

http://ethics.aaanet.org/category/statement/
http://www.nybooks.com/articles/archives/2000/feb/10
https://www.opendemocracy.net/beyondslavery/alice-bellagamba/legacies-of-slavery
    -in-southern-senegal.
http://www.oralhistory.org/about/do-oral-history/oral-history-and-irb-review/
http://www.oxfordaasc.com/article/opr/t338/e0209
http://www.tandfonline.com/doi/abs/10.1080/0144039X.2015.1008213#
http://www.thevillageofhope.com/

Ghana Public Records and Archives Administration (GPRAA)—Accra
(full citations in endnotes)

ADM 1–
ADM 11–
ADM 12–
ADM 39–
ADM 41–
SC 12/6–
SC 14–

Ghana Public Records and Archives Administration Regional Office at Ho

Item No. 14, Case No. 5.82: Haussa Community—John Maxwell, Commissioner of the
    Eastern Province, Quittah, to the Honorable Colonial Secretary, Accra, 8 October
    1909.

District Court Grade II, Anloga, Ghana

Judicial Council Minute Book, 1913
Judicial Council Record Book, 1914

Anlo Traditional Council Office, Anloga, Ghana

Anlo State Council Minute Book, 1935

Staatasrchiv, Bremen, Germany

Bremen Staatasrchiv: 7, 1025–

Oral Interviews

Greene, Sandra E. Field Note 52: Interview with Dzobi Adzinku, 15 December 1987, Anloga.
———. Field Note 53: Interview with Afatsao Awadzi, 16 December 1987, Anloga.
———. Field Note 54: Interview with Tse Gbeku, 16 December 1987, Anloga.
———. Field Note 57: Interview with Robert G. Kofi Afetogbo, 22 December 1987, Anloga.
———. Field Note 59: Interview with Amawota Amable, 23 December 1987, Anloga.
———. Field Note 60: Interview with Tete Za Agbemako, 5 January 1987, Anloga.
———. Field Note 63: Interview with L. A. Banini, 5 January 1988, Anloga.
———. Field Note 69: Interview with Dzobi Adzinku, 7 January 1988, Anloga.
———. Field Note 70: Interview with Kwami Kpodo, 12 January 1988, Woe.
———. Field Note 72: Interview with Christian Nani Tamakloe, 13 January 1988, Keta.
———. Field Note 74: Interview with A. W. Kuetuade-Tamaklo, 19 January 1988, Tegbi.
———. Field Note 77: Interview with Kwami Kpodo, 20 January 1988, Woe.
———. Field Note 91: Interview with Amegashie Afeku IV, 18 February 1988, Accra-Nima.
———. Field Note 92: Interview with Amegashie Afeku IV, 19 February 1998, Accra-Nima.
———. Field Note 96: Interview with Anthonio Gbordzor II and his councilors, 24 February 1988, Woe.
———. Field Note 97: Interview with J. W. Kodzo-Vordoagu, 24 February 1988, Tegbi.

Index

Page numbers in *italics* refer to figures and tables.

SANDRA E. GREENE is the Stephen '59 and Madeline '60 Professor of African History at Cornell University. Her single-authored books include *Gender, Ethnicity, and Social Change on the Upper Slave Coast* (Heinemann, 1996), *Sacred Sites and the Colonial Encounter* (IUP, 2002), and *West African Narratives of Slavery* (IUP, 2011). Her co-edited collections include the five-volume *New Encyclopedia of Africa* (Thomson/Gale, 2008), which won the Conover Porter Prize, *African Voices on Slavery and the Slave Trade, Vols. 1 and 2* (Cambridge, 2013, and 2016), and *The Bitter Legacy: African Slavery Past and Present* (Markus Wiener Press, 2013). She is also the author of many articles in various journals and edited collections. Her research has been supported most recently by Cornell University, the National Humanities Center (where she held the John Hope Franklin Senior Researcher Fellowship), and by the Mellon Foundation. In addition to writing and teaching courses on African and African Diaspora history, she has served in a number of administrative positions including Chair of the History Department at Cornell and President of the African Studies Association (USA).

CPSIA information can be obtained
at www.ICGtesting.com
Printed in the USA
BVHW041824240620
582238BV00016B/1227